RAND LABOR AND POPULATION

T0288892

The Effects of Travel and Tourism on California's Economy

A Labor Market–Focused Analysis

Matthew D. Baird, Edward G. Keating, Olena Bogdan, Adam C. Resnick

For more information on this publication, visit www.rand.org/t/RR1854

Library of Congress Cataloging-in-Publication Data is available for this publication
ISBN: 978-0-8330-9736-1

Published by the RAND Corporation, Santa Monica, Calif.

© Copyright 2017 RAND Corporation

RAND® is a registered trademark.

Cover: GettyImages/davemantel.

Support RAND

Make a tax-deductible charitable contribution at
www.rand.org/giving/contribute

www.rand.org

Preface

Visit California, a 501(c)6 nonprofit corporation formed in 1998 to market California as a desirable tourism destination, asked the RAND Corporation to estimate the effects of travel/tourism on the state's economy. Visit California works in close coordination with California's Division of Tourism; the organization conducts marketing programs that drive visitation, while the Division of Tourism oversees the assessment program that helps fund these initiatives. Visit California operates under the auspices of the Governor's Office of Business and Economic Development (GO-Biz). The GO-Biz director serves as chairperson of the organization. RAND was asked to prepare a study using data on California tourism and California's labor force to provide insight about who works in tourism in California and how these individuals' careers evolve.

This report should be of interest to policymakers and researchers interested in economic development issues and labor force career pathways.

This research was undertaken within RAND Labor and Population. RAND Labor and Population has built an international reputation for conducting objective, high-quality, empirical research to support and improve policies and organizations around the world. Its work focuses on children and families, demographic behavior, education and training, labor markets, social welfare policy, immigration, international development, financial decisionmaking, and issues related to aging and retirement with a common aim of understanding how policy and social and economic forces affect individual decisionmaking and human well-being.

For more information on RAND Labor and Population, contact the unit director: Unit Director, RAND Labor and Population, 1776 Main Street, P.O. Box 2138, Santa Monica, CA 90407-2138, (310) 393-0411, or visit the Labor and Population website at www.rand.org/labor.

Contents

Figures

Tables

Summary

The State of California attracts hundreds of millions of visitors annually. The travel/tourism industry generates revenue for businesses and tax revenue for the state and local governments and provides employment to hundreds of thousands of Californians.

In this report, we focus on the travel/tourism industry labor market in California—that is, how travel/tourism affects the workers in California employed in the industry. Generally, we find that travel/tourism employs a diverse workforce that contributes meaningfully to California's economy. For some, travel/tourism is a career path with stability, good wages, and wage growth; for others, it is a transitional industry, often providing access to the paid labor force for those not coming from previous employment.

It is not always obvious which workers in California are employed in travel/tourism. There are some workers who are universally categorized as working in the industry (e.g., airline employees, amusement park employees, hotel employees, museum employees, sightseeing operators). Even for those workers, however, there is ambiguity: A portion of visitors to a museum, for instance, is from the local area and does not count as travelers or tourists.

There are other workers, such as restaurant employees and retail employees, whose jobs depend in part on travelers. For many restaurants and stores, customers are a mix of local, non-traveler customers and customers visiting the area.

Given that our focus is on workers in the industry and how their careers evolve, we must simplify and categorize any given worker as either employed in California's travel/tourism industry or not. We focus on workers most squarely in the travel/tourism industry and describe how their careers evolve. Our baseline travel/tourism definition includes transportation services (e.g., air, rail, car rentals), accommodations (e.g., hotels), entertainment (e.g., museums), amusement, gambling, and some other smaller categories incidental to travel/tourism (e.g., recreational vehicle parks and camps). We evaluate the sensitivity of our industry definition by looking at a borderline case where workers are partially influenced by travel/tourism (i.e., workers employed by eating and drinking establishments).

The RAND Corporation's methodology in this report is data-centered—that is, we analyzed data describing who worked in California's travel/tourism industry. The analysis provides insight about how travel/tourism contributes to the careers of its workers.

Basic Statistics About the Travel/Tourism Industry in California

Our analysis is built on four different U.S. Census Bureau–collected data sources: the American Community Survey (ACS), the Current Population Survey (CPS), Quarterly Workforce

Indicators (QWI), and the Survey of Income and Program Participation (SIPP). SIPP is of particular interest to us because it follows the same individuals over multiple years. These data sources were developed for different reasons, measuring similar things but employing different methodologies. Both because of methodological differences and inherent statistical random-ness, these data sources provide different point estimates of, for instance, the level of travel/tourism employment in California. However, we find that these four data sources are generally mutually reinforcing and cross-validating for our analysis.

Focusing on travel/tourism-related employment in California, the four data sets suggest that roughly 800,000 workers had their primary employment in the industry between 2009 and 2013. Travel/tourism, as we have defined it, encompasses about 4.5 percent of California's civilian labor force. Travel/tourism employment is spread across a number of constituent indus-tries with "amusement, gambling, and recreation industries" being the largest single employ-ment subcategory, with about 30 percent of California's travel/tourism employment, as we have defined it.

We find that about one-third of California travel/tourism workers worked fewer than 35 hours per week, a higher non-full-time fraction than observed in California's overall labor force.

While hourly wages in the industry have been, on average, lower than nontravel/tourism workers' hourly wages, there is a right tail of higher-wage travel/tourism workers. More than one-quarter of California's travel/tourism workers earn $20 or more per hour.

The age profile of California's travel/tourism workers has been fairly evenly spread, but there is a concentration of workers in their early 20s.

Industry employment can be bifurcated between long-term and transitional employees. The former spend lengthy stretches employed in travel/tourism, while the latter use it as a launching point into other industries. Long-term employees in travel/tourism are almost a decade older than the transitional employees, work almost four more hours per week, and earn more than $5 more per hour than the transitional employees in travel/tourism. Each of these differentials is near or at the top in relation to our comparison industries.

Data Describing Entrants into and Separators Away from California's Travel/Tourism Industry

There has been fairly considerable churn into and out of California's travel/tourism indus-try. Our data sources estimate that roughly 200,000 workers have entered and a correspond-ing number have separated away from the industry annually between 2009 and 2013. About 30 percent of California travel/tourism workers were new to the industry in a typical year.

SIPP data suggest that, of entrants into the industry between 2010 and 2013, almost 40 percent were not in the paid labor force the year preceding. The plurality of these new-to-the-paid-labor-force workers was in school the year preceding, but the industry also hired a number of workers who were unemployed or not in the labor force. In 2010–2013, travel/tour-ism had a larger percentage of its entrants come from outside of the paid labor force than was true of other, comparably sized industries in California.

About two-thirds of those who separated from travel/tourism moved to employment in a different industry. Eleven percent of travel/tourism industry separators entered school, a higher percentage than observed for other, comparably sized industries in California.

Fifteen percent of California travel/tourism workers who moved to a job in a different industry increased their hourly wage by at least 50 percent. This percentage was comparable with other industries.

Supplemental Analyses

To a first approximation, California's travel/tourism workers have been demographically similar to travel/tourism workers nationwide, although California's workers are more likely to be Hispanic or Asian. California's travel/tourism industry has drawn a larger percentage of new workers from outside of the paid labor force than has been the case nationwide.

If one includes California's restaurants and bars in travel/tourism, the industry is, on average, considerably younger and lower paid. In 2010–2013, with this expanded industry definition, an even greater percentage of new workers came from outside of the paid labor force (predominantly from school). Also, a greater percentage of individuals who separated from the industry moved to a considerably more lucrative job in a different industry.

Use of an earlier SIPP panel (2004–2007 rather than 2009–2013) finds that California's travel/tourism industry hired more people before the recession, but drew fewer new workers from outside of the paid labor force. The explanation for this finding could be that California had a much lower unemployment rate in 2004–2006 (averaging 5.5 percent) than it had in 2009–2012 (11.3 percent). Hence, when the state's economy was performing better, more new travel/tourism workers were drawn away from employment in other industries.

Acknowledgments

We thank Dan Mishell and his colleagues Ryan Becker, Caroline Beteta, Lynn Carpenter, and Angie Pappas at Visit California for sponsoring this research and assisting in its development.

We thank Gary Buffo of Pure Luxury Transportation, Dean Runyan and Bill Klein of Dean Runyan Associates, Adam Sacks of Tourism Economics, and Tien X. Tian of the U.S. Travel Association for insights about the travel/tourism industry.

We thank RAND Labor and Population program director Krishna Kumar for his considerable enthusiasm and support. We also thank Marvin Bonta, Michael Dworsky, John Engberg, Esther Friedman, Charles Goldman, Andrew Hoehn, Katherine Lee, Susan Marquis, Erik Meijer, Joy Moini, Kathleen Mullen, Lance Tan, Liz Voss, Donna White, Benson Wong, and Christopher Young of RAND.

Jim Hosek of RAND provided ongoing constructive review of this research. We also received a constructive review from an anonymous reviewer. M. Rebecca Kilburn coordinated RAND's quality-assurance process for this project. Sarah Bana provided a number of suggestions that improved this report.

We also thank Justin Adams and Daniel Sommerhauser for their assistance.

Abbreviations

ACS	American Community Survey
ASEC	Annual Social and Economic Supplement [to the CPS]
BEA	Bureau of Economic Analysis
CGE	computable general equilibrium
CPS	Current Population Survey
GSP	gross state product
IMPLAN	Impact Analysis for Planning
IO	input-output
LEHD	Longitudinal Employer-Household Dynamics
NAICS	North American Industry Classification System
QWI	Quarterly Workforce Indicators
RIMS	Regional Input-Output Modeling System
SIPP	Survey of Income and Program Participation
TSA	tourism satellite account

CHAPTER ONE

Introduction

The State of California has attracted roughly 250 million person trips annually since 2014; 2015 saw 263 million trips.[1] Dean Runyan Associates estimated total direct travel spending in California was $117.5 billion in 2014 and $122.5 billion in 2015;[2] U.S. Travel Association estimated statewide total travel expenditures of $124 billion in that year.[3] The travel/tourism industry generates revenue for businesses in the state as well as tax revenue for state and local government.[4] It also provides employment for hundreds of thousands of Californians.

In this report, we focus on the labor-market effects of travel/tourism. Who is employed in the industry? Where did they come from? How long do they stay in the industry? Where do they go after working in the industry? The effect of the industry is not restricted to the period individuals work in it. Additionally, experience in the industry can affect the labor-market outcomes of its alumni.

This report is not a policy analysis or evaluation. Rather, our purpose is descriptive—that is, to better understand the role California's travel/tourism industry plays in the careers of its workers.

It is not obvious which workers in California are employed because of travel/tourism. There are some workers who are universally categorized as working in the industry. These include airline employees, amusement park employees, hotel employees, museum employees, and sightseeing operators. Even for those workers, however, there is ambiguity: A portion of

---

[1] Tourism Economics, "California Travel and Tourism Outlook" briefing, February 2016, slide 5.

[2] Dean Runyan Associates, *California Travel Impacts, 1992–2014p*, Portland, Oreg., April 2015.

[3] U.S. Travel Association, *The Impact of Travel on State Economies: 2015 Edition*, Washington, D.C., January 2016b.

[4] The United Nations notes

> Tourism as a demand-side phenomenon refers to the activities of visitors and their role in the acquisition of goods and services. It can also be viewed from the supply side, and tourism will then be understood as the set of productive activities that cater mainly to visitors. A visitor is a traveller [sic] taking a trip to a main destination outside his/her usual environment for less than a year and for any main purpose (business, leisure or other personal purpose) other than to be employed by a resident entity in the country or place visited. (United Nations, *Tourism Satellite Account: Recommended Methodological Framework 2008*, Luxembourg, Madrid, New York, and Paris: Department of Economic and Social Affairs, Statistics Division, Studies in Methods Series F, No. 80/Rev. 1, 2010)

Under this definition, a business traveler counts as a tourist. We therefore use the phrasing "travel/tourism" to make clear that we are including all travelers, including business travelers, in our analysis scope. Tourism Economics finds that roughly 80 percent of annual person trips to California are for leisure and 20 percent for business (Tourism Economics, 2016). Nationwide, U.S. Travel Association (2016b) estimated $645.3 billion in leisure travel spending (70 percent) and $282.8 billion in business travel spending (30 percent) in 2014.

visitors to a museum, for instance, is from the local area and does not count as travelers or tourists.[5]

There are other workers, such as restaurant employees and retail employees, whose jobs depend, in part, on travelers. For many restaurants and stores, customers are a mix of local, nontraveler customers and customers visiting the area. The U.S. Travel Association estimates that travelers accounted for 26.8 percent of all spending on food service and drinking places in the United States in 2014.[6] Of course, the traveler percentage varies with a restaurant's location (e.g., a restaurant near Disneyland most likely draws more than 26.8 percent of its revenue from travelers).

Travel/tourism is not an industry as defined by the North American Industry Classification System (NAICS). Rather, travel/tourism is an activity that draws on different NAICS codes (e.g., 7211 [traveler accommodations], 481111 and 481211 (passenger air transportation], 712 [museums, historical sites, and similar institutions]).

The United Nations uses the vernacular "tourism satellite account" (TSA) to reflect the fact that tabulating the economic effect of tourism requires drawing from multiple underlying industry codes, as tourism is itself not such a code.[7] Douglas Frechtling notes that "the TSA is a 'satellite' to a larger body, in this case the system of national accounts. . . . As a satellite, it must define its major outputs ('macroeconomic aggregates') in reference to those that are defined and measured"[8] by the internationally adopted system of national accounts (e.g., NAICS).

In this report, we break methodologically from approaches employed by Dean Runyan Associates and the U.S. Travel Association.[9] Both sources use what we will term a *travel vector expenditure approach*. Estimates are made on how much a typical traveler spends and across which categories. Then, in conjunction with an estimate of the number of travelers coming to the state, estimates are provided on the total spending of these travelers across myriad categories. There are categories in the travel vector expenditure approach—such as gasoline stations, where traveler spending is considerable—that are dwarfed by local resident spending.

A methodology that attributes fractions of a worker's activities to travel/tourism is useful in many cases,[10] but does not allow for examinations of transitions into and out of an industry. Our transition-based methodology requires single-industry classifications. We assign each worker to only one industry (e.g., is the worker's job predominantly within California's travel/tourism industry?). We then examine the career paths of individuals we categorize as primarily employed in California's travel/tourism industry. What were they most typically doing before working in the travel/tourism industry? Where did they go after employment in the industry?

Because our methodology focuses on individual workers' careers, we need to categorize any given worker as either employed in California's travel/tourism industry or not. We are not

---

[5]   U.S. Travel Association (2016b, p. 72) defines *travel* as activities associated with all overnight and day trips to places 50 miles or more away, one-way, from the traveler's origin and any overnight trips away from home in paid accommodations.

[6]   U.S. Travel Association, 2016b.

[7]   United Nations, 2010.

[8]   Douglas C. Frechtling, "The Tourism Satellite Account: A Primer," *Annals of Tourism Research*, Vol. 37, No. 1, January 2010, pp. 136–153.

[9]   Dean Runyan Associates, 2015; and U.S. Travel Association, 2016b.

[10]   Such as those used by Dean Runyan Associates, 2015, and U.S. Travel Association, 2016b.

concerned with subtle or borderline cases in which a worker is partially influenced by travel/ tourism. Rather, we focus on workers most squarely in the travel/tourism industry and describe how their careers evolve. Our methodology does not cover as many employees or as large a dollar value as the travel vector expenditure approach. But we gain insight on career trajectories of individuals who work most unequivocally in California's travel/tourism industry.

In Table 1.1, we enumerate the NAICS codes we include in California's travel/tourism industry as well as six large codes we exclude from our definition. We built Table 1.1 using our judgment, but also used NAICS codes we saw typically included under the travel/tourism

Table 1.1
Categories of Workers Included and Excluded from Our Definition of California's Travel/Tourism Industry

Included	2012 NAICS Code
Air transportation	481
Rail transportation	482
Water transportation	483
Taxi and limousine service	4853
Scenic and sightseeing transportation	487
Support activities for transportation	488
Automotive equipment rental and leasing	5321
Travel arrangements and reservation services	5615
Performing arts, spectator sports, and related industries	711
Museums, art galleries, historical sites, and similar institutions	712
Amusement, gambling, and recreation industries	713, excluding 71395[a]
Traveler accommodation	7211
Recreational vehicle parks and camps	7212
Rooming and boarding houses	7213

Examples of Excluded	
Full-service restaurants	7221
Limited-service eating places	7222
Drinking places	7224
Gasoline stations	447
Retail	Various (44* and 45*)
Urban transit systems	4851

[a] NAICS code 71395 is for bowling centers that we assume are largely frequented by local residents.

rubric in others' analyses.[11] But none of these categories is pure. Plenty of local residents attend performing arts events while travelers clearly eat at restaurants, for instance.

In a labor market–focused analysis such as this, researchers must differentiate between *jobs* and *workers*. A given worker can hold more than one job. Hence, there will be more jobs than workers.

In focusing on workers, as we do in this analysis, researchers must next decide which job(s) are of interest. One could analyze any job the worker holds or one might wish to focus on a worker's most important or primary job. Our analysis uses only each worker's primary job, which will tally fewer total jobs than one that encompasses all jobs. Likewise, such labor-market metrics as average wages and average hours worked will have different values based on which job(s) one considers.

For the purpose of this study, we focus on workers whose primary job in a given year (defined as the job they spent the most total time in that year) is in California's travel/tourism industry. We further categorize each person in each year into either working, in school, unemployed, or out of the labor force, depending on the category in which he or she spent the most months.[12] We will not include fractional workers using a spending vector; in fact, we are unable to do so, as we will be looking at transitions into and out of the industry, wage evolutions, and overall career trajectories, which depend on binary definitions of inclusion into or exclusion from the industry. Given our different focus and methodology, our estimates will be different than other reports on California travel/tourism (e.g., Dean Runyan Associates'). This does not mean that either set of estimates is wrong, only that they are reporting different things.

The remainder of this report is structured as follows: In Chapter Two, we present basic statistics about the travel/tourism industry in California, drawing on four different U.S. Census Bureau–collected data sources. These data describe employees in the industry (e.g., their ages, their wages). We categorize workers as belonging to the travel/tourism industry or not and use the data sources to compare these workers with groups of workers in other industries in California. Chapter Three presents data describing entrants into and separators away from California's travel/tourism industry. Where did entrants come from, and where did separators go? Are these patterns different for travel/tourism compared with other comparably sized California industries? Chapter Four presents supplemental analyses. In particular, we examine how results change if one uses national (not California-only) data, if one uses a more-inclusive definition of who works in the industry (adding restaurant industry workers), or if one uses an earlier panel of worker data. Chapter Five provides a concluding discussion. In the appendix, we discuss input-output (IO) economic-impact models that are often used to assess the effect of the travel/tourism industry.

---

[11] M. Delgado, M. E. Porter, and S. Stern, *Defining Clusters of Related Industries,"* June 2014; U.S. Travel Association, *The Economic Review of Travel in America: 2015 Edition*, Washington, D.C., January 2016a; U.S. Travel Association, 2016b; Dean Runyan Associates, *California Travel Industry: Business Characteristics, Employees, Wages*, Portland, Oreg., May 2013.

[12] In case of a tie, individuals are categorized as working.

CHAPTER TWO

Basic Statistics About the Travel/Tourism Industry in California

Data Sources

Our analysis relies most centrally on the U.S. Census Bureau's Survey of Income and Program Participation (SIPP). However, as cross-validation for certain statistics, we additionally use three other data sets. Each of the four different data sources was developed for different reasons, measuring similar elements but employing different methodologies.

The primary SIPP panel we use surveyed the same people quarterly from September 2008 through December 2013 (i.e., it tracked specific individuals for five years and three months). SIPP interviewees were queried quarterly. However, each quarterly interview included questions about labor-market behavior in each of the three months preceding. Therefore, SIPP reports monthly data.

SIPP is uniquely good for measuring career transitions. Of particular interest to us, by having repeated surveys of the same individuals, we can see where tourism/travel industry employees came from, where they went when they left the industry, and how their wages changed as they entered into and separated away from the industry. There were 122,184 unique individuals in this SIPP panel, with 10,835 respondents who lived in California at some point during the panel. SIPP uses national weights to make this sample of 122,184 individuals representative of the national adult population in the United States; we take the subset of the data for California and use these national weights.[1] We collapsed the data to annual measures both for direct comparison with our other data sources and to more accurately reflect the transitions we are interested in: primary jobs held in a year. The final analytic data set contains 399,537 person/year observations, 37,803 of which are in California.

We use three other data sets to supplement our insights from the SIPP. The U.S. Census Bureau's American Community Survey (ACS) is an annual survey sent to roughly 3.5 million households (approximately one in every 38 households), supplanting what had been the "long form" of the decennial census. We use the Public Use Microdata Sample, a subsample of the larger ACS that is available to all researchers. We also only use data for California. This sample provides us with roughly 300,000 individual responses per year. ACS's primary value to us is

---

[1] SIPP provides several nationally representative weights for use in the SIPP, but no California weights. We used these national SIPP weights for two reasons: first, so that weights are consistent across samples and models (i.e., when we estimate California samples or when we estimate national samples), and second, for additional confidence by using the Census-generated weights that take into account many complicated facets of the data and sampling, which we were unprepared to generate for a California-specific sample. See U.S. Census Bureau, *Quarterly Workforce Indicators 101*, Washington, D.C., December 18, 2015, for details on the weighting. The first-best solution would be having subset-specific weights, but using overall weights for a subset of the weighted population (such as, in our case, a given state) is common in practice and should improve on not using any weights.

in being an order-of-magnitude validation of estimates from the SIPP. ACS's very large number of observations helps assure us that the trends that appear in data sets with smaller sample sizes are not merely statistical noise. In the ACS, workers are not followed over time, so we cannot chart career changes using this data source.

The Current Population Survey (CPS) is a monthly snapshot of the labor force jointly sponsored by the U.S. Census Bureau and the U.S. Bureau of Labor Statistics. We focus, in particular, on the March Annual Social and Economic Supplement (ASEC) to the CPS. The survey has approximately 150,000 respondents each year and approximately 15,000 annual respondents in California. The March ASEC asks a number of questions, such as about annual income, that are of value to us. The CPS is good for estimating the number of workers in an industry and how much they were paid, but is not well suited to tracing career histories, since the same people are not tracked month to month.

The U.S. Census Bureau's Quarterly Workforce Indicators (QWI) are a set of economic markers that include employment, job creation, earnings, and other measurements of employment flows. As the name implies, these data are quarterly, not monthly. These data are not individual responses to surveys, but are instead generated from administrative records. The source data for the QWI are the Longitudinal Employer-Household Dynamics (LEHD)–linked employer-employee microdata. The LEHD data set is a massive longitudinal database covering over 95 percent of U.S. private-sector jobs. While it provides estimates drawing from much of the working population, including transition data, the underlying microdata are unavailable to us to investigate for more-specific trends.[2] In addition, by using administrative records, there will be a lack of representation of jobs that are undocumented or self-employed, which is not necessarily true for the other three survey-based data sets.[3]

These four data sources provide somewhat different estimates of any given statistic. One reason is that the surveys use different methodologies, reflecting their different purposes. The ACS uses large samples to obtain accurate snapshots, but does not interview over time. The CPS accepts smaller samples in the interest of timeliness. SIPP interviews specific individuals over time at the cost of having a smaller sample. As samples, ACS, CPS, and SIPP estimates all include sampling variability. QWI obtains timely data covering almost every worker in the United States, but without any interviews and at the cost of omitting self-employed and undocumented employees.

We wanted our data sources to be comparable with one another. ACS and ASEC (to the CPS) data are annual. We annualized the monthly SIPP by taking the respondent's job that was reported for the most cumulative hours across the year as his or her primary job. In our usage of the SIPP, a given worker is tied to a single job, the job with the most hours worked, even if he or she held multiple jobs either concurrently or sequentially in a year. This may differ from what people reported as their primary job in the ACS or CPS. The ACS asks about the current job (which is thus likely to include more transitory positions), while the CPS asks about the primary job across the past year. Even if they think over the past year, the respondents may unconsciously put more weight on recent jobs.

QWI uses a count of all workers in each industry that has been observed in the same job for three consecutive quarters. A job is marked as a stable job in the middle quarter, as the

---

[2]   See U.S. Census Bureau, 2015.

[3]   The other three surveys are randomly sampled respondents, which may draw from undocumented worker populations.

worker is guaranteed to have started the middle quarter and ended the middle quarter in that same job. This is not necessarily the same as what we think of as the primary job in a year; a worker could have a job be his or her primary job if he or she had six jobs, each for one month, and a seventh job for two months, but none of these would be counted as a stable job for QWI purposes. Given this, QWI's stable-job construct is similar to, but not the same as, the primary annual jobs in the CPS and SIPP. Not surprisingly, therefore, job tallies vary across these data sources.

Worker Demographics

Table 2.1 presents demographic characteristics of four working populations: travel/tourism workers in California, all workers in California, travel/tourism workers in the nation overall, and all workers in the nation. These statistics are based on the 2009–2013 SIPP. The travel/tourism industry in California employs a diverse group of workers. For example, travel/tourism employs racial groups that approximately mirror the diverse group of employees in California as a whole. Travel/tourism has workers from every education group. Both in California and nationwide, travel/tourism workers compared with workers overall have been

- more likely to be male
- slightly younger
- less likely to be married
- less likely to have children under age 18
- less likely to be college graduates.

Levels of Employment and Gross State Product

Travel/tourism is an important industry in California, in terms of both employment and generated gross state product (GSP). Figure 2.1 shows estimates of the number of travel/tourism workers in California between 1991 and 2015 from the QWI. QWI, as noted, provides counts of what it terms *stable jobs*. We average the quarterly estimates by year to remove seasonality and to get an overall annual plot that mirrors the other data sets we use.[4]

The 2008–2009 Great Recession is readily apparent in Figure 2.1, with a sharp dip of approximately 100,000 workers employed in the industry during this period. Notwithstanding the 2008–2009 downturn, the long-term trend has been one of growth in employment in California's travel/tourism industry. Recall that, by not using a spending-vector approach that yields fractional employment in various industries and by focusing only on those whose primary job in a year is in the industry, our estimates will be lower than those employing more liberal definitions. In spite of the tight definition of travel/tourism, we find that travel/tourism employs a large number of workers in California, over 800,000 annually across the last 15 years, and that number is growing.

---

[4] Seasonality can be important in the travel/tourism industry. If an individual only works in the industry during the summer and is a full-time student during the school year, that individual would count as a student, thereby understating the importance of travel/tourism.

Table 2.1
Worker Characteristics in the SIPP, California and Nationally, 2009–2013

	California		Nation	
	Travel/Tourism	All Workers	Travel/ Tourism	All Workers
Age (average)	38.51	39.81	39.63	40.47
Male (%)	57.0	53.8	57.0	51.5
Race				
African American (%)	5.1	6.3	13.4	11.9
Asian (%)	13.7	11.9	5.5	4.3
Other non-white (%)	2.6	4.2	4.3	3.3
Hispanic (%)	36.2	35.0	16.2	14.9
Education				
High school or less (%)	35.8	31.6	36.3	32.5
Some college (%)	36.9	35.4	40.2	36.2
College graduate (%)	27.3	33.0	23.5	31.3
Individuals in household (average)	3.52	3.46	3.12	3.17
Lives in metropolitan area (%)	96.6	95.8	82.1	80.3
Owns house (%)	56.7	56.2	62.7	67.2
Has children under age 18 (%)	62.7	71.7	58.2	68.5
U.S. citizen (%)	83.2	84.2	91.1	91.8
Speaks language other than English (%)	40.1	39.5	19.9	17.8
Married (%)	47.2	54.1	44.2	53.1
Has previously retired (%)	3.9	3.7	5.6	4.6
Observations in SIPP	884	18,188	8,761	197,740

SOURCE: SIPP, 2009–2013.

In 2013, California's civilian labor force was estimated to include about 18.6 million individuals,[5] and travel/tourism represented about 4.5 percent of that total. California's civilian labor force, as the name implies, excludes members of the U.S. military. It also excludes retirees, full-time students, and other individuals not currently looking for work. It includes employed civilians as well as unemployed, but actively looking, individuals.

Table 2.2 uses SIPP data to compare travel/tourism worker employment, wage, and hours worked data to eight "comparison industries": (1) administrative/support/waste management,[6] (2) agriculture, (3) construction, (4) durable manufacturing, (5) education, (6) financial activi-

---

[5] U.S. Department of Labor, "Economy at a Glance: California," undated(b).

[6] The awkward label "administrative/support/waste management" is nomenclature used in the NAICS. Quoting U.S. Department of Labor:

Figure 2.1
Estimated Travel/Tourism Employment in California, 1991–2015

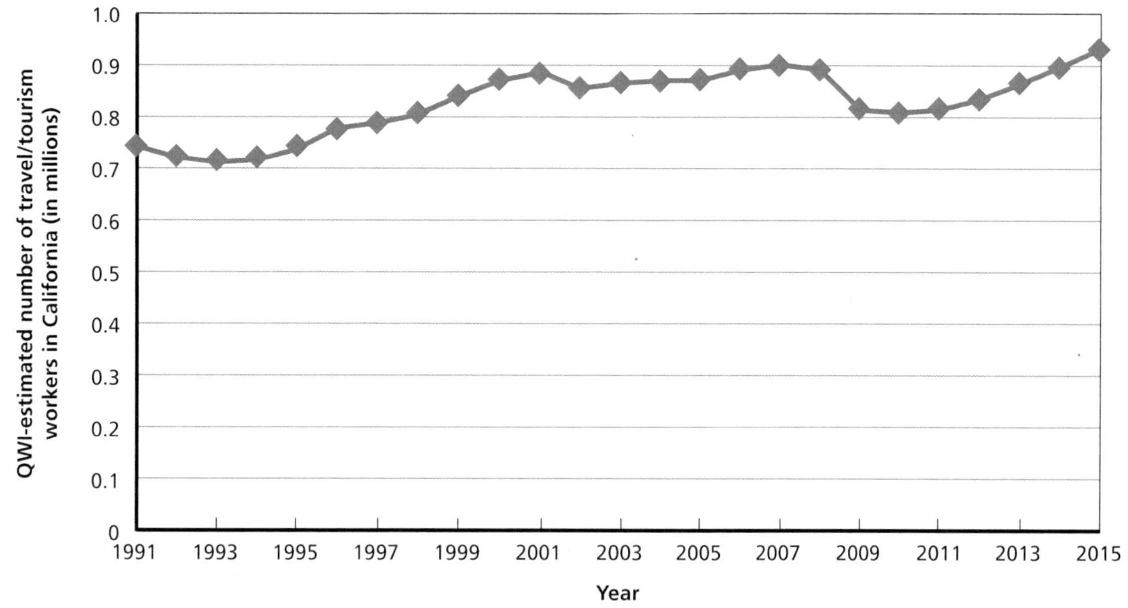

SOURCE: QWI, 1991–2015.
RAND RR1854-2.1

ties, (7) transportation/warehouse/utilities,[7] and (8) wholesale trade. These industries provide important comparisons for the role that travel/tourism plays in the California economy.[8] Thus, to choose the comparison industries, we used the two-digit NAICS industry codes and estimated in the SIPP the fraction of employed individuals in each of these industries. We then chose the eight industries with the closest share of employed workers in California to travel/tourism.

We use the eight comparison industries to provide context to various statistics we provide describing California's travel/tourism industry. A value such as the percentage of new workers who came from outside of the paid labor force (a statistic we use heavily below) lacks any obvious meaning except when put in comparison with other industries' values of the same statistic.

In the 2009–2013 SIPP, California's travel/tourism employment level was closest to that of admin/support, construction, and financial activities. The workers in these industries also

---

The Administrative and Support and Waste Management and Remediation Services sector comprises establishments performing routine support activities for the day-to-day operations of other organizations. These essential activities are often undertaken in-house by establishments in many sectors of the economy. The establishments in this sector specialize in one or more of these support activities and provide these services to clients in a variety of industries and, in some cases, to households. Activities performed include: office administration, hiring and placing of personnel, document preparation and similar clerical services, solicitation, collection, security and surveillance services, cleaning, and waste disposal services. (U.S. Department of Labor, Bureau of Labor Statistics, "Administrative and Support and Waste Management and Remediation Services: NAICS 56," January 6, 2017a)

[7] Transportation excludes, however, the transportation-related NAICS codes we are including in our definition of travel/tourism.

[8] As many of the trends we are interested in depend on transitions into and out of an industry, it is essential that the comparison industries be of comparable sizes. Choosing an industry that is significantly larger leads to lower transition rates in and out of such an industry as a result of its larger size, making our comparisons less informative.

Table 2.2
Employment, Wage, and Hours Worked Data for Travel/Tourism and Comparison Industries in California, 2009–2013

Industry	Workers in California (Thousands)	Average Wage ($)	Average Age	Average Weekly Hours	Percentage Part-Time
Travel/tourism	772	19.64	39	35	31
Administrative/support/ waste management	802	16.06	38	37	23
Agriculture	288	11.69	38	41	14
Construction	724	23.38	40	39	18
Durable manufacturing	1,167	27.23	42	41	7
Education	1,740	25.90	43	35	32
Financial activities	746	30.52	40	41	10
Transportation/warehouse/ utilities	592	22.42	42	41	11
Wholesale trade	520	22.73	42	40	12
Statewide	16,423	23.00	40	37	23

SOURCE: SIPP, 2009–2013.

had similar average ages. However, the average wages in construction and financial activities were considerably higher than in travel/tourism ($23.38 and $30.52 versus $19.64), while the administrative/support/waste management industry's average wage was lower ($16.06). Travel/tourism had the second largest share (after education), 31 percent, of part-time workers across the comparison industries.

Spanning a longer period (1991–2015), Figure 2.2 juxtaposes travel/tourism employment in California with QWI-estimated employment levels in the state for the eight comparison industries.

Figure 2.2 shows a long-term decline in durable manufacturing employment in California with education and, later, admin/support having surpassed its employment level. California's travel/tourism industry in 2015 had approximately the same employment level as the state's construction industry, but construction-employment levels have been far more volatile.

The U.S. Bureau of Economic Analysis (BEA) provides estimates of the GSP associated with industries in California. Figure 2.3 shows that travel/tourism, as we have defined it, neared $80 billion in annual GSP in the state in 2014. In 2014, California's GSP was estimated to be $2.3 trillion;[9] travel/tourism, as we define it, represented about 3.4 percent of that total. Dean Runyan Associates estimates California's travel/tourism GSP to be at $62.3 billion in 2015,[10] about 2.5 percent of the California total GSP. Not knowing

---

[9]   U.S. Department of Commerce, Bureau of Economic Analysis, "Broad Growth Across States in 2014," Washington, D.C., June 10, 2015.

[10]   Dean Runyan Associates, *California Travel Impacts by County, 1992–2015p*, Portland, Oreg., April 2016.

Figure 2.2
Estimated Travel/Tourism Employment in California Compared with Selected Other Industries, 1991–2015

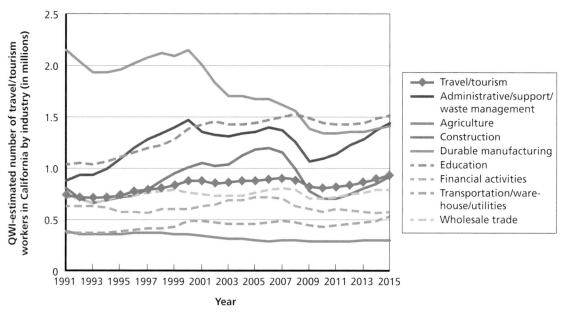

SOURCE: QWI, 1991–2015.

RAND *RR1854-2.2*

Figure 2.3
Estimated Travel/Tourism Annual GSP in California, 1997–2014

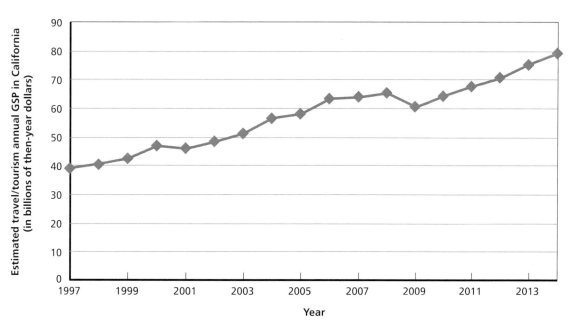

SOURCE: BEA, 1997–2014.

RAND *RR1854-2.3*

the company's source of data nor its definition of the industry, it is unclear why our estimates are larger.

In addition, Dean Runyan Associates and the U.S. Travel Association calculate total revenue, which, as opposed to GSP, includes the value of intermediate inputs, and thus will be larger than GSP estimates. As noted at the beginning of Chapter One, travel vector–based approaches estimate greater travel/tourism contributions. Thus, our estimates are below the revenue-spending vector estimates of Dean Runyan Associates' $117.5 billion and U.S. Travel Association's $124 billion.[11]

As was true in Figure 2.1's depiction of travel/tourism employment levels over time, the long-term trend in travel/tourism GSP in California has been favorable, notwithstanding the 2008–2009 downturn.

Paralleling Figure 2.2, Figure 2.4 compares travel/tourism GSP with other industries' GSP levels in California.

As was true with employment levels, travel/tourism GSP in 2014 was very close to construction GSP in California, but construction GSP has been far more volatile. Travel/tourism GSP in California has risen in close parallel to admin/support GSP. While California's durable manufacturing employment level has fallen to be only the third highest of the nine industries in Figure 2.2, durable manufacturing remains the highest GSP of the nine industries in Figure 2.4.

Figures 2.1–2.4 show data back to the 1990s. Not all of our data sets go back as far. Figure 2.5 presents 2009–2013 estimates of California travel/tourism employment levels from SIPP and the three other data sources (QWI, ACS, and CPS).

While the estimates presented in Figure 2.5 are somewhat different from one another, we view the four sources as estimating roughly the same magnitude of travel/tourism employment in California.

The ACS provides the highest estimated employment level perhaps because it asks about the respondent's current job, even if he or she only holds it for one week. The other three data sources try to focus on stable jobs. The presence of transitional employees in travel/tourism could additionally explain higher count estimates from the ACS than the other three data sources.

Using travel vector methodologies, the U.S. Travel Association estimates travel-generated employment of 933,600 in California in 2014,[12] while Dean Runyan Associates estimates travel-generated employment in the state of 1,027,000 in 2014.[13] For 2013, the average of our four data sets is 845,000. However, we stress again that this is not a fair comparison, and we are not suggesting that the other, higher estimates are too high. Instead, they are measuring different things: for example, measuring jobs instead of workers (workers may hold multiple jobs), including peripheral industry jobs through spending vectors (which we do not include) and perhaps including transitory jobs (while we try to focus on more stable jobs).

---

[11] See Dean Runyan Associates, 2015, and U.S. Travel Association, 2016b. These larger, travel vector–based estimates are arguably better estimates of the contribution generated by travel/tourism in California. Our more-conservative conception of the industry is driven by our labor market focus (i.e., our desire to track the careers of individual workers). Our GSP tally in Figure 2.3 does not, for instance, include traveler spending at restaurants.

[12] U.S. Travel Association, 2016b.

[13] Dean Runyan Associates, 2015.

Figure 2.4
**Estimated Travel/Tourism Annual GSP in California Compared with Selected Other Industries,
1997–2014**

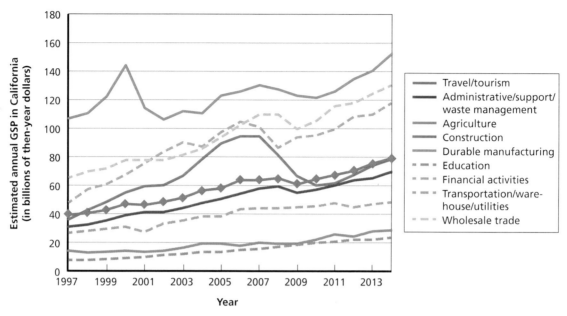

SOURCE: QWI, 1997–2014.

RAND *RR1854-2.4*

Figure 2.5
Estimated Annual Travel/Tourism Employment Levels in California, 2009–2013

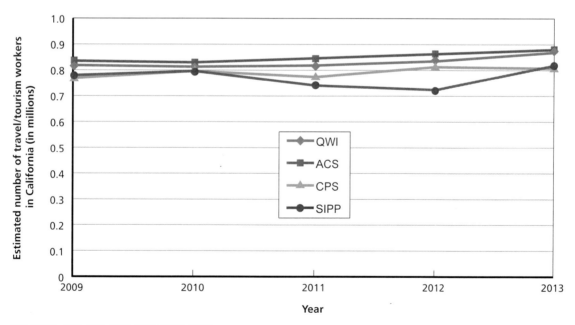

SOURCES: ACS, CPS, QWI, SIPP, 2009–2013.

RAND *RR1854-2.5*

Using the SIPP, we find there are at least two types of workers employed in the travel/tourism industry in California: long-term employees, who tend to stay for longer, are older, and have higher wages; and transitional employees, who may use the industry as a launching point into the workforce. Both of these types of career paths are of value not only to travel/tourism, but to the California economy. While travel/tourism is not unique in that respect, it is in some respects more bifurcated than the comparison industries. For example, in the SIPP, the percentage of workers employed every year in travel/tourism out of those employed any of the five years in the industry is 45.2 percent.[14] This almost evenly splits the workforce. Interestingly, this ratio is approximately in the middle among the comparison industries, which have values ranging from 29.8 percent to 64.4 percent (Table 2.3). Travel/tourism's position in the middle of this distribution compared with the other industries supports the idea of travel/tourism more uniquely offering both career paths.

Table 2.3
Comparison of Long-Term Versus Transitional Workers by Industry

Industry	Percentage of Workers Employed Each Year in the Industry	Average Wage Difference[a] ($)	Average Weekly Hours Worked Difference[a]	Average Age Difference[a]
Travel/tourism	45.2	5.10	3.5	9.9
Administrative/support/waste management	29.8	2.00	0.1	5.2
Agriculture	53.1	1.58	7.8	8.9
Construction	53.6	4.63	0.3	4.0
Durable manufacturing	54.9	3.46	1.8	6.8
Education	64.4	3.33	3.6	7.1
Financial activities	55.4	9.62	2.8	5.2
Transportation/warehouse/utilities	55.4	4.68	0.6	5.4
Wholesale trade	38.5	3.64	0.6	4.8

SOURCE: SIPP, 2009–2013.
NOTE: The SIPP data are restricted to individuals who worked each of the five years of the sample. Each row is additionally restricted to workers who were employed in the industry labeled, in at least one of the five years.
[a] Differences refer to the average value for those employed each of the five years of the sample in the industry labeled versus those employed less than five but at least one year of the sample in the industry labeled.

---

[14] We limit the sample of individuals to those present in each of the five years of the SIPP sample to make the argument for long-term employment stronger.

Wages, Hours, and Ages

We also use the other data sets to cross-validate SIPP-estimated average wages in travel/tourism and nontravel/tourism in California.[15] As shown in Figure 2.6, across the ACS, CPS, and SIPP, travel/tourism had a lower average wage over 2009–2013 than nontravel/tourism.[16] This finding is consistent with other research. For example, Lacher and Oh estimated that jobs generated by tourism expenditures in coastal regions of South Carolina have a lower income distribution than average in the regions.[17]

The ACS and SIPP average wage estimates are very close to each another; the CPS estimate is higher for both industry groups. However, even with the differences in tourism average wage for the CPS, the 95-percent confidence intervals (denoted by the error bars) overlap each other for the SIPP and the other two data sets for travel/tourism average wages (i.e., the average wages are not statistically different across the three data sets). Not surprisingly, standard errors are much smaller for nontravel/tourism, as each of the data sources has much-larger sample sizes with which to estimate the average wage outside of California's travel/tourism industry.

Overall, the three data sets in Figure 2.6 tell a similar story regarding wages—that travel/tourism has paid a below-average wage to its workers in California. However, we again found evidence for a separation between career travel/tourism workers and transitional employees, shown in Table 2.3. Those who worked all five years in travel/tourism earn on average $5.10 more in hourly wage than those who worked all five years in any of the nine industries but

Figure 2.6
Average Wages in California Across Data Sources, 2009–2013

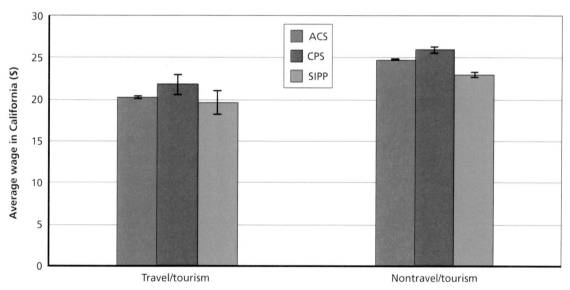

SOURCES: ACS, CPS, and SIPP, 2009–2013.
RAND RR1854-2.6

---

[15] We use the term *nontravel/tourism* to encompass all workers in California except those we define to work in California's travel/tourism industry. Of course, there are vastly more nontravel/tourism workers than there are travel/tourism workers.

[16] QWI does not provide hourly wage estimates.

[17] R. Geoffrey Lacher and Chi-Ok Oh, "Is Tourism a Low Income Industry? Evidence from Three Coastal Regions," *Journal of Travel Research*, Vol. 51, No. 4, July 2012, pp. 464–472.

with at least one of those years being in travel/tourism. This is the second-highest differential, after the financial activities industry. On the lower end is the agriculture industry, where the difference is $1.58 per hour.

Figure 2.7 provides a 2009–2013 SIPP pie chart of the number of employees associated with the NAICS codes we attribute to California's travel/tourism industry.

The three largest categories are amusement, gambling, and recreation industries (NAICS 713, excluding 71395), traveler accommodation (7211), and support activities for transportation (488). "Support activities for transportation" includes such establishments as air traffic control services, marine cargo handling, and motor vehicle towing.[18]

Figure 2.7's categories correspond to NAICS codes; as a satellite account, we define the "travel/tourism industry" as the union of these underlying industries.

We next examine the distribution of weekly hours worked in and out of the travel/tourism industry. Figure 2.8 breaks up weekly hours of work into five-hour brackets.

For almost every five-hour bracket below 40 hours per week, travel/tourism had a higher percentage of workers than nontravel/tourism, while for every bracket above 40 hours per week, nontravel/tourism had a higher percentage of workers than travel/tourism. About one-third of California travel/tourism workers worked fewer than 35 hours per week. In contrast,

Figure 2.7
California Travel/Tourism Workers by NAICS Code, 2009–2013

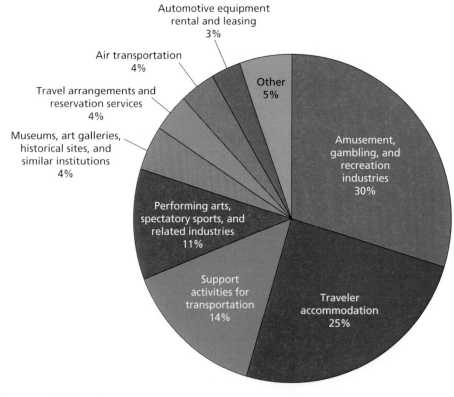

SOURCE: SIPP, 2009–2013.
RAND RR1854-2.7

---

[18] U.S. Department of Labor, Bureau of Labor Statistics, "Support Activities for Transportation: NAICS 488," January 6, 2017b.

Figure 2.8
Distribution of California Workers' Weekly Hours of Work Inside and Outside of Travel/Tourism, 2009–2013

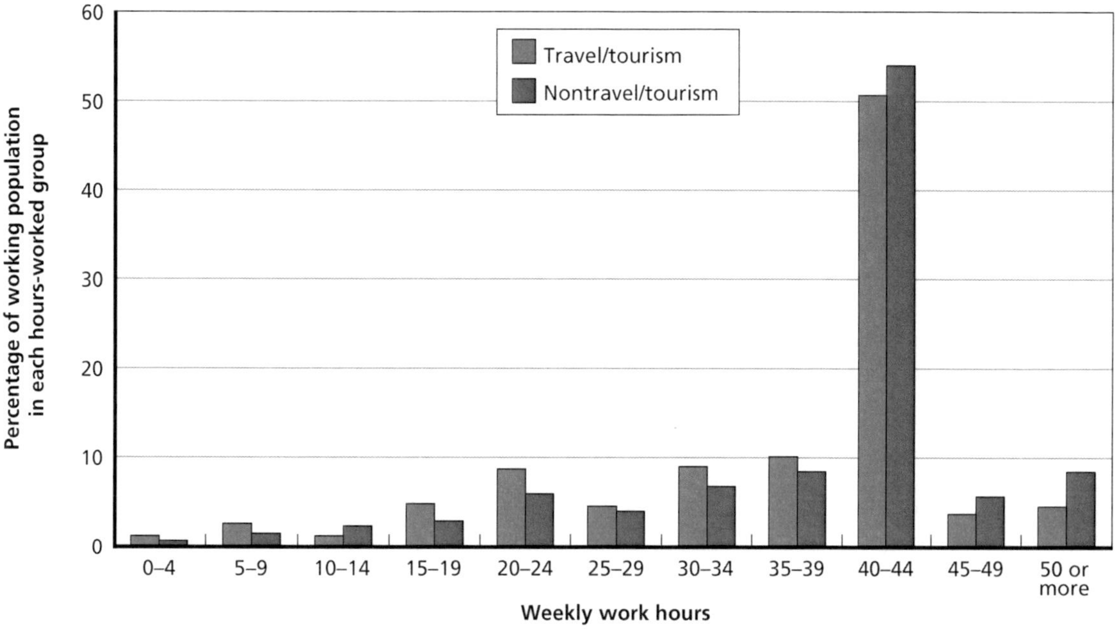

RAND *RR1854-2.8*

of nontravel/tourism workers in California, only about one-quarter worked fewer than 35 hours per week. However, even within travel/tourism, the highest percentage of workers in any bracket was between 40 and 44 hours per week, with 50.4 percent representing California's travel/tourism workers.

Those who worked all five years in travel/tourism worked on average 3.5 more hours per week than those who worked all five years in any of the nine industries, with at least one of those years being in travel/tourism (but not all of the years). This is the third-highest differential among our comparisons (Table 2.3), after agriculture and education. On the lower end is the admin/support industry, where the difference is 0.1 hours a week (or roughly no difference).

Figure 2.9 shows the age distribution of California's travel/tourism industry versus other industries in the state.

Large differences occur before age 40. For example, 25 percent of travel/tourism workers were younger than 25 years old, while only 14 percent of nontravel/tourism workers were younger than 25. Other researchers have also found that tourism has a relatively youthful workforce.[19] We again see potential differences between long-term employees and transitional employees. Those who worked all five years in travel/tourism were, on average, 9.9 years older than those who worked all five years in any of the nine industries, with at least one of those years being in travel/tourism, but not all of the years. This is the highest differential among our comparisons (Table 2.3). On the lower end is the construction industry, where the difference is four years of age.

---

[19] Rosemary Lucas, *Employment Relations in the Hospitality and Tourism Industries*, London: Routledge, 2004.

Figure 2.9
Distribution of California Workers' Ages Inside and Outside of Travel/Tourism, 2009–2013

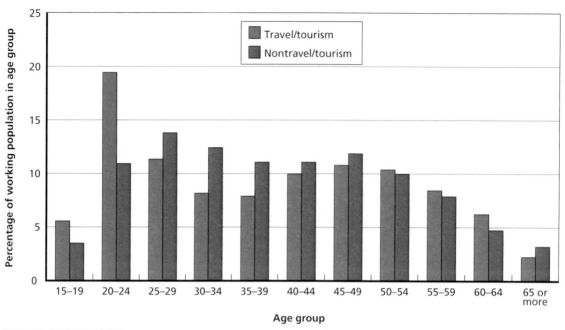

SOURCE: SIPP, 2009–2013.
RAND RR1854-2.9

We next turn to estimates of earnings. Because of the prevalence of fractional employment we presented in Figure 2.8, we will not present annual earnings data that do not separate out the rate of pay from the hours of work. Instead, hourly wages allow us to control for differences in hours worked each week. Interviewees in the SIPP were asked about their hourly wage and monthly earnings for their jobs. About half of respondents who were working had a nonmissing, nonzero response only for both hourly wage and monthly earnings. Forty percent of SIPP respondents entered a response only for monthly wages and 10 percent only for hourly wage rate. We use the hourly wage rate reported for the 60 percent who reported an hourly wage. For the remaining 40 percent, we impute their hourly wage by multiplying the monthly earnings from the job by 12 divided by 50 (to approximate weekly earnings) and then dividing by their reported average weekly hours. A further problem is that the hourly wage is censored at $35 per hour in the SIPP—that is, all individuals with wages more than $35 per hour were recorded as $35 per hour. We replace the hourly wage rate with the imputed wage rate if the hourly wage rate is the censored value of $35. It appears that the resulting imputed wage and adjusted hourly wage for individuals who reported both are similar, with averages within about a dollar of each other. If the resulting wage estimate was below $8 per hour, we set it equal to $8 per hour.[20] Finally, we take wages exceeding the top 99.9th percentile of wages and set it

---

[20] California's minimum wage during this period was $8 per hour (State of California, Department of Industrial Relations, "History of California Minimum Wage," January 1, 2016).

equal to the top 99.9th percentile, a trimming exercise commonly used to control for measurement error.[21]

As shown in Figure 2.10, while hourly wages in the travel/tourism industry were low for some workers, there is a right tail of higher wage earners (as is true in other industries).

Twenty-eight percent of California travel/tourism workers earned $20 or more per hour, and 41 percent of California travel/tourism workers earned $15 or more per hour. These percentages are less than the 42 percent of California's nontravel/tourism workers who received $20 or more per hour and 58 percent who received $15 or more per hour. The SIPP estimates that the average wage for travel/tourism workers was about $19.50 per hour, while nontravel/tourism workers averaged $23 per hour. However, median hourly wages were substantially

Figure 2.10
Distribution of California Workers' Hourly Wages Inside and Outside of Travel/Tourism, 2009–2013

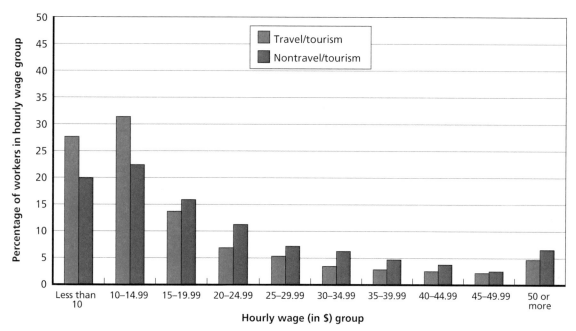

SOURCE: SIPP, 2009–2013.
RAND RR1854-2.10

[21] See, for example, among many papers that follow this practice, Audra J. Bowlus and Shannon N. Seitz, "Search Friction in the U.S. Labor Market: Equilibrium Estimates from the PSID," *Contributions to Economic Analysis*, Vol. 243, 2000, pp. 145–170; David McKenzie, Caroline Theoharides, and Dean Yang, "Distortions in the International Migrant Labor Market: Evidence from Filipino Migration and Wage Responses to Destination Country Economic Shocks," *American Economic Journal: Applied Economics*, Vol. 6, No. 2, 2014, pp. 49–75; Brahim Boudarbat and Marie Connolly, "The Gender Wage Gap Among Recent Post Secondary Graduates in Canada: A Distributional Approach," *Canadian Journal of Economics/Revue canadienne d'économique*, Vol. 46, No. 3, August 2013, pp. 1037–1065; and Jeremy Lise, Nao Sudo, Michio Suzuki, Ken Yamada, and Tomoaki Yamada, "Wage, Income and Consumption Inequality in Japan, 1981–2008: From Boom to Lost Decades," *Review of Economic Dynamics*, Vol. 17, No. 4, 2014, pp. 582–612. For a discussion of trimming wage outliers in data, see Alexander Whalley, "Education and Labor Market Risk: Understanding the Role of Data Cleaning," *Economics of Education Review*, Vol. 30, No. 3, 2011, pp. 528–545; Jason W. Osborne and Amy Overbay, "The Power of Outliers (and Why Researchers Should Always Check for Them)," *Practical Assessment, Research, and Evaluation*, Vol. 9, No. 6, March 2004, pp. 1–12; and Milan Terek and Matús Tibenský, "Outliers and Some Non-Traditional Measures of Location in Analysis of Wages," *European Scientific Journal*, Vol. 1, September 2014, pp. 480–486.

lower: $12.50 per hour for travel/tourism workers and $17 for nontravel/tourism workers in California.

Figure 2.10's hourly wages do not adjust for experience, age, and education level, all of which vary considerably across workers. The difference in wages between travel/tourism and nontravel/tourism workers is driven in part by travel/tourism having younger, less-educated workers more frequently working in less-than-full-time jobs.

Summary

Our analysis relies most centrally on the Survey of Income and Program Participation, a U.S. Census Bureau–collected panel that surveyed the same people quarterly between September 2008 and December 2013.

Travel/tourism employment in California averaged about 800,000 in 2009–2013, or about 4.5 percent of the state's civilian labor force. About one-third of California travel/tourism workers worked fewer than 35 hours per week. Workers under age 25 have been overrepresented in the industry. While there is a right tail of higher-wage earners in California's travel/tourism industry, average and median wages in travel/tourism have been lower than observed for nontravel/tourism workers in the state.

We bifurcate California's travel/tourism labor force between long-term employees and transitional employees who use the industry as a career launching point. Long-term employees in travel/tourism are almost a decade older than the transitional employees, work almost four more hours per week, and earn over $5 more per hour than the transitional employees in travel/tourism. Each of these differentials is near or at the top in relation to our comparison industries.

Data Describing Entrants into and Separators Away from California's Travel/Tourism Industry

Suppose that we observe an individual accepting a job in the travel/tourism industry. We infer that he or she is better off because of the job, as evidenced by his or her accepting it. We do not know, however, what the individual's next-best alternative would have been (i.e., the opportunity cost of the individual working in the travel/tourism industry). Perhaps the individual would have been working in a different industry absent the travel/tourism job. Alternatively, perhaps the individual would have otherwise not been in the paid labor force (e.g., in school, unemployed, not in the labor force).[1]

If the new travel/tourism worker would have otherwise been working in a different industry, the question arises how that "travel/tourism alternative" industry responded to the absent worker. Perhaps that industry hired someone else (from yet another industry or perhaps from outside of the paid labor force). Or perhaps the travel/tourism alternative industry simply reduced its employment level.

A new travel/tourism job may result in a net societal increase in employment (if someone is hired from outside of the paid labor force, either directly by travel/tourism or eventually by an alternative industry), or it may simply result in a reallocation of employment as some alternative industry commensurably declines. Either way, the new travel/tourism job has increased societal welfare as the worker voluntarily accepted it (assuming the worker maximizes his or her present and future payoff), but we do not know whether net societal employment has increased.

The examination of new entrants and separators is further a natural extension of our earlier findings of evidence of there being different types of workers: long-term workers in travel/tourism who do stay in the industry and transitional workers who only work in the travel/tourism industry for a short period and may use it as a launching pad.

In this chapter, we examine these granular questions by looking at entrants into California's travel/tourism industry as well as separators out of the industry. Where did workers new to the industry come from? Where did workers who separated away from the industry go? Do age and earnings differ depending on whether the new entrants came from a different industry or from outside the paid labor force? What can we infer about the opportunity cost of employment in California's travel/tourism industry?

---

[1] The rubric *not in the labor force* applies to individuals who do not have jobs and are not in school, but do not count as being unemployed. To count as being unemployed, an individual must be actively seeking work. *Not in the labor force* individuals include retirees, stay-at-home parents, as well as "discouraged workers," who are no longer actively seeking paid employment.

Data on Entrants and Separators

Figure 3.1 shows that there has been fairly considerable churn into and out of California's travel/tourism industry.[2]

Upward of 200,000 workers entered the industry, and a roughly corresponding number separated away from it annually between 2010 and 2013. Note that we are tallying entrance into and separation away from the industry. Changing *jobs* within the travel/tourism industry is not tallied as a transition.

While Figure 3.1 shows SIPP data, it is heartening to note that the QWI provides broadly similar estimates of hires into and separations out of California's travel/tourism industry in these years. The SIPP methodology relies on both an estimate of the proportion that enters into and separates away from the industry each year as well as an estimate of the size of the industry's population. QWI comes from administrative records and just records the number of transitions between industries each quarter; summing up over a year provides an estimate of total entrances and separations. For example, for 2013, SIPP estimates entrances of 237,000 workers into travel/tourism while QWI estimates 230,000; SIPP estimates separation of 173,000 workers while QWI estimates 208,000. Although other years have slightly larger deviations, the deviations are always of the same magnitude. The largest deviation is for 2009 to 2010 separations, where SIPP estimates 276,000 workers and QWI estimates 197,000 workers.

Comparing travel/tourism to the eight comparison industries, Figure 3.2 shows the percentage of each industry's workforce that was new to the industry in a typical year (e.g., work-

Figure 3.1
Estimated Annual Entrants into and Separators Away from California's Travel/Tourism Industry, 2010–2013

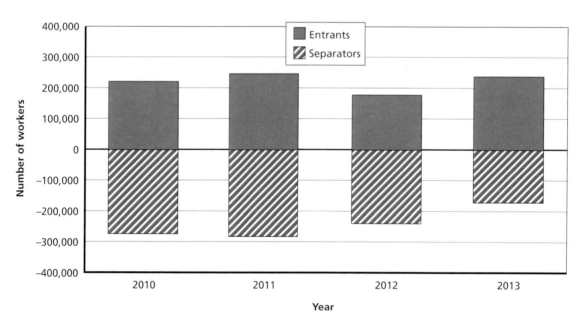

SOURCE: SIPP, 2009–2013.
NOTE: 2009 is the base year for calculations.
RAND RR1854-3.1

---

[2] Figure 3.1 employs an expositional convention that we will use throughout the remainder of this report: Displays associated with entrants are in a solid color; displays associated with separators use diagonal stripes.

Figure 3.2
Average Annual Percentage of Entrance and Separation for Comparison Industries, 2010–2013

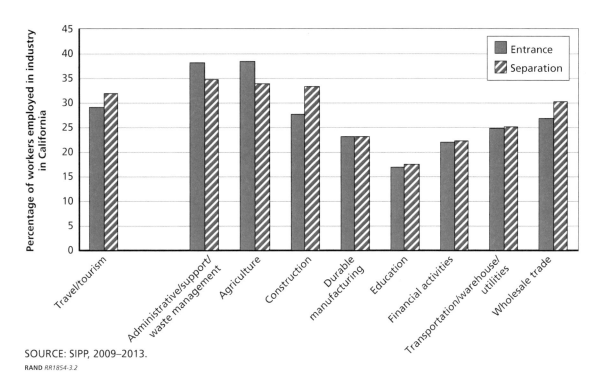

SOURCE: SIPP, 2009–2013.
RAND *RR1854-3.2*

ing in the industry in 2013, but not in 2012) as well as the percentage that separated away from the industry in a typical year (e.g., working in the industry in 2012, but not in 2013). Figure 3.2 averages annual hiring and separation rates over 2010–2013.

Travel/tourism had the third-highest entrance rate and fourth-highest separation rate across the nine industries in California. Admin/support and agriculture had higher entrance and separation rates than travel/tourism. California's education industry had the lowest annual turnover rates of these nine industries for 2010–2013.

The SIPP data can tell us where entrants into California's travel/tourism industry worked in the year preceding. Between 2010 and 2013, as shown in Figure 3.3, almost 40 percent of workers new to California's travel/tourism industry were not in the paid labor force the year preceding.

Figure 3.3 shows that 39 percent of entrants into travel/tourism came from outside of the paid labor force (or, put differently, 61 percent were employed in a different industry the year before beginning employment in travel/tourism). Deconstructing the 39 percent who came from outside of the paid labor force, 16 percent were unemployed, 16 percent were in school, and 8 percent were not in the labor force the year prior.[3]

Among our comparison industries, for 2010–2013, travel/tourism had the highest percentage of new employees who came from outside of the paid labor force (39 percent), with wholesale trade having the smallest percentage across the nine industries (27 percent).[4]

---

[3] Values do not add to 39 percent because of rounding.

[4] Travel/tourism's 39-percent value in Figure 3.3 is statistically significantly greater than the previous-year not-in-the-paid-labor-force rates for transportation/warehouse/utilities and wholesale trade at the 5-percent significance level. It is

Figure 3.3
Previous-Year Status of Entrants into Comparison Industries in California, 2010–2013

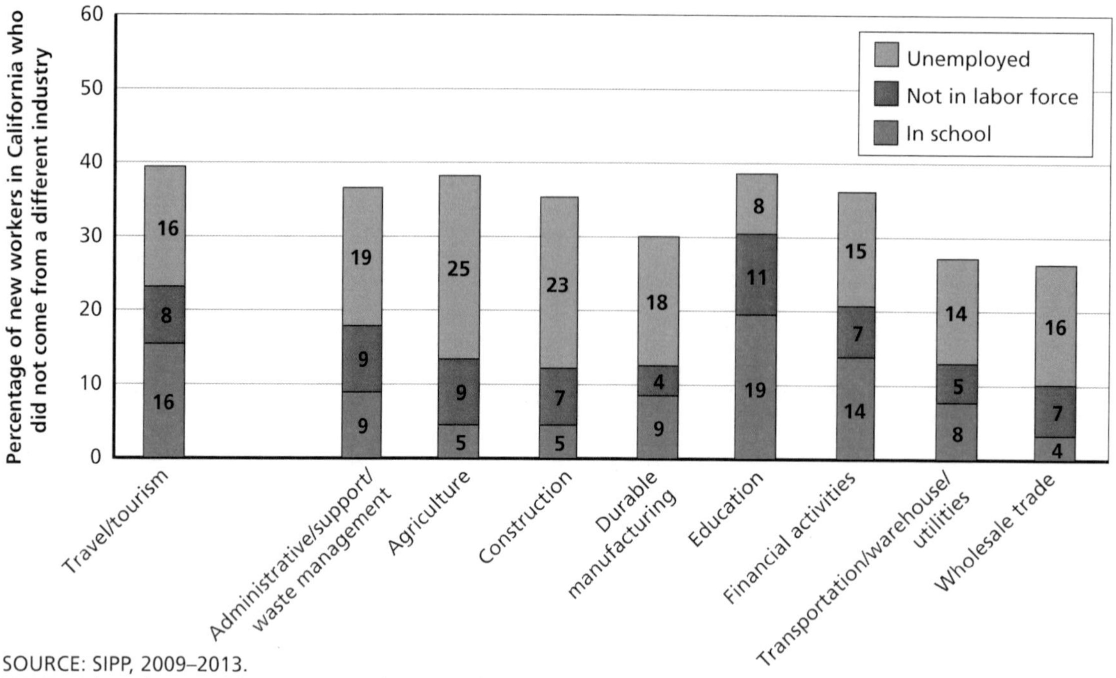

SOURCE: SIPP, 2009–2013.
NOTE: Values do not add to 39 percent because of rounding.
RAND RR1854-3.3

One implication of Figure 3.3 is that California's travel/tourism industry has been welcoming to individuals not currently in the paid labor force. The industry appears to have comparatively low barriers to entry for new workers, absorbing entrants at a higher rate than the comparison industries. This finding is consistent with Szivas, Riley, and Airey's research suggesting that the tourism industry contains a diverse set of jobs accommodating different worker skills.[5] At the same time, other industries with higher turnover rates (such as admin/support) seem to draw more of their new workers from the existing labor force pool (i.e., workers moving between industries).

It is also useful to understand the demographics of workers who entered each industry. Figure 3.4 shows the percentage of 2010–2013 entrants into the different industries who were under age 30.

More than 50 percent of entrants into California's travel/tourism industry were under 30 years old, a higher percentage than observed in any of the comparison industries.

Both the relatively youthful age profile of the industry (Figure 2.9 in Chapter Two and Figure 3.4) and the sizable number of entrants from outside of the paid labor force (Figure 3.3) are consistent with Dean Runyan Associates' observation that the travel industry is well-suited

---

greater than the durable manufacturing rate at the 10-percent significance level. For the other five categories, the SIPP sample sizes were too small for the observed rate differences to be statistically significant. All tests are based on a regression of an indicator for coming from outside of the paid labor force (in the sample of all industry entrants) on a set of indicators for each industry, with travel/tourism the reference group.

[5] Edith Szivas, Michael Riley, and David Airey, "Labor Mobility into Tourism: Attraction and Satisfaction," *Annals of Tourism Research*, Vol. 30, No. 1, 2003, pp. 64–76.

Figure 3.4
Age Distribution of Entrants into Comparison Industries in California, 2010–2013

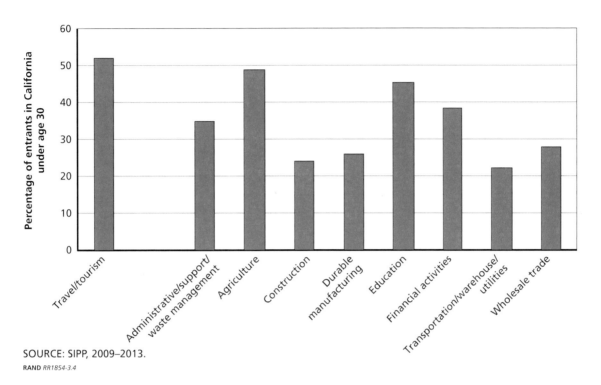

SOURCE: SIPP, 2009–2013.

RAND *RR1854-3.4*

to providing opportunities to the unemployed and to individuals entering the workforce.[6] Further, younger workers in travel/tourism are more likely to come out of the paid labor force conditional on entering: The average age of new entrants coming from outside the paid labor force is 28 years old, compared with 33 years old for new entrants coming from a different industry. This difference of five years is the third largest among the comparison industries, after transportation/warehouse/utilities and education industries (see Table 3.1).

Figure 3.5 describes the educational background of entrants into the industries.

About 60 percent of entrants into California's travel/tourism industry had some college experience (a categorization that includes some college and college graduates). Travel/tourism entrants, on average, have been less likely to have college experience than entrants into California's education and financial activities industries, but much more likely to have college experience than entrants into California's agriculture industry. Further, workers with lower education in travel/tourism are more likely to come out of the paid labor force conditional on entering: 17 percent of new workers in travel/tourism coming from outside the paid labor force had bachelor's degrees, compared with 31 percent of new entrants coming from a different industry. This difference is the second largest among the comparison industries, after wholesale trade (Table 3.1). This again suggests two potentially different career paths in travel/tourism: the long-term worker and the transitional worker.

Whereas Figure 3.3 shows that travel/tourism has had a larger percentage of its entrants come from outside of the paid labor force than observed in the comparison industries, about 66 percent of those who separated from travel/tourism moved to employment in a different

---

[6] Dean Runyan Associates, 2013.

Table 3.1
Difference in Age and Percentage with BA/BS Degrees for New Industry Entrants Coming from Outside Paid Labor Force Versus Those Coming from Other Industries

Industry	Age Difference of Entrants	Different in Entrants with BA/BS Degree (%)
Travel/tourism	−5.02	−13
Administrative/support/waste management	−1.72	−13
Agriculture	6.22	−6
Construction	2.58	6
Durable manufacturing	0.11	−9
Education	−5.64	−11
Financial activities	−3.12	−7
Transportation/warehouse/utilities	−9.71	0
Wholesale trade	−2.04	−15

SOURCE: SIPP 2010–2013, new entrants into the industry.

Figure 3.5
Educational Backgrounds of Entrants into Comparison Industries in California, 2010–2013

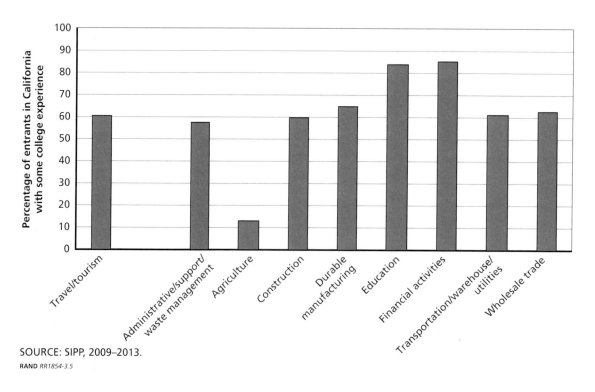

SOURCE: SIPP, 2009–2013.
RAND *RR1854-3.5*

industry, or, put differently, 34 percent were not in the paid labor force the year after they left California's travel/tourism industry. Figure 3.6 shows that travel/tourism's separator rate of not being in the paid labor force was broadly typical.

California's education and, especially, agriculture industries have had much higher percentages of their separators leave the paid labor force. For 2010–2013, travel/tourism had the highest proportion of entrants coming from outside of the paid labor force among these comparison industries (Figure 3.3) but was typical in the rate of its separators leaving the paid labor force (Figure 3.6).

Separators from California's travel/tourism industry were more likely to attend school the next year (11 percent of industry separators) than was true of any of the comparison industries. This highlights the younger ages of many travel/tourism workers, who were able to use travel/tourism as an opportunity to enhance their skill sets plus build up funds to pay for additional education.

Figure 3.7 presents the distribution of ratios of individuals' new hourly wage to their old hourly wage averaged across 2010 to 2013. We estimate the distribution for three different groups: those who entered travel/tourism from a different industry (not in travel/tourism last year but are this year), those who stayed in travel/tourism (those who were in travel/tourism last year and this year), and those who separated away from travel/tourism but are employed in a different industry (those who were in travel/tourism last year but not this year). The blue bars in Figure 3.7 do not include individuals who were not employed the year preceding; the red bars likewise do not include individuals not employed after employment in travel/tourism.

Note the large spike at stable wages (100–109 percent of last year's wage) for those who stayed in California's travel/tourism industry. Many of those who stayed in the industry stayed

Figure 3.6
Year-After Status of Separators Away from Comparison Industries in California, 2010–2013

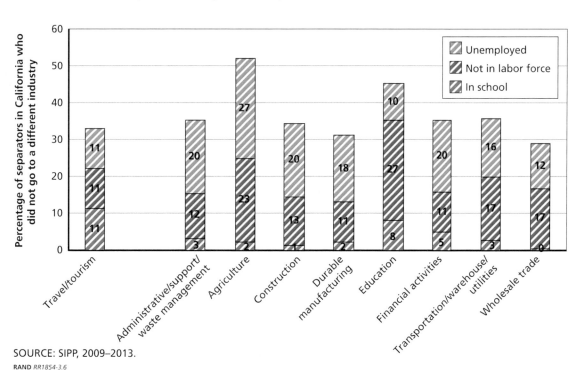

SOURCE: SIPP, 2009–2013.
RAND *RR1854-3.6*

Figure 3.7
Average Change in Wages from Previous Year in California Travel/Tourism, 2010–2013

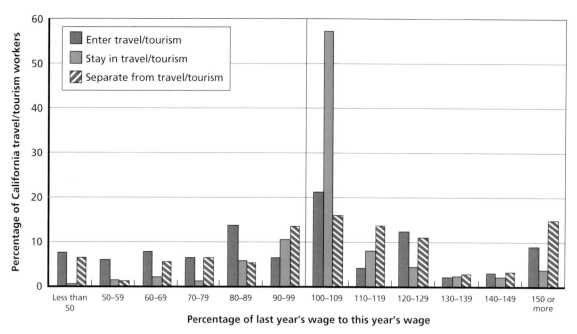

SOURCE: SIPP, 2009–2013.

RAND *RR1854-3.7*

in the same job. Insofar as individuals often change jobs to increase wages, this spike implies that those who stayed in California's travel/tourism industry generally had slower growth in wages than those who changed industries. For both entrants into and separators away from travel/tourism, there is a large group of individuals with a more than 50-percent increase in wages (150 percent or more of previous wage), but that group was larger for separators. This result again suggests that younger, less-experienced, and less-educated workers may be able to use travel/tourism as a springboard for their careers.

While the median change in hourly wage for workers transitioning from travel/tourism to a different industry is a 1.8-percent wage increase, 15 percent of individuals who moved to a job in a different industry increased their hourly wage by 50 percent or more. This sort of favorable outcome is consistent with the sanguine arguments of U.S. Travel Association that travel-related jobs provide a path to upward mobility.[7] Roger Dow of the U.S. Travel Association noted, "I know firsthand how important travel jobs can be, from the skills they provide to the opportunities they create and the doors they open."[8] However, 37 percent of those who left California's travel/tourism industry for a job in a different industry received less per hour than their travel/tourism job paid. While travel/tourism can be a stepping stone to a higher-paid position in a different industry, such a favorable outcome is not guaranteed.

---

[7]   U.S. Travel Association, *Fast Forward: Travel Creates Opportunities and Launches Careers*, Washington, D.C., 2012.

[8]   U.S. Travel Association, 2012, p. 2.

The fact that 15 percent of travel-industry separators who moved into employment in a different industry received hourly wage increases of 50 percent or more is, in fact, typical across our comparison industries, as shown in Figure 3.8.

Travel/tourism has been, if anything, on the low end of the percentage of its separators receiving large wage increases.

Figure 3.9 complements this analysis by estimating average wage changes associated with transitions by industry.[9]

As one might expect, the average change for those who stayed in an industry (and likely in the same job) was modest (i.e., about a 5-percent wage increase). Average wage growth was higher for most industry switchers. For those who entered California's travel/tourism industry, average wage growth that year was slightly negative. This result echoes the observation in Figure 3.7 that almost one-half (48 percent) of entrants into travel/tourism had experienced a wage decrease from their previous employment. This is consistent with Szivas and Riley's portrayal of travel/tourism sometimes playing a refuge role for workers leaving declining indus-

Figure 3.8
Percentage of Employed Industry Separators Receiving
50-Percent-or-Larger Wage Increase, 2010–2013

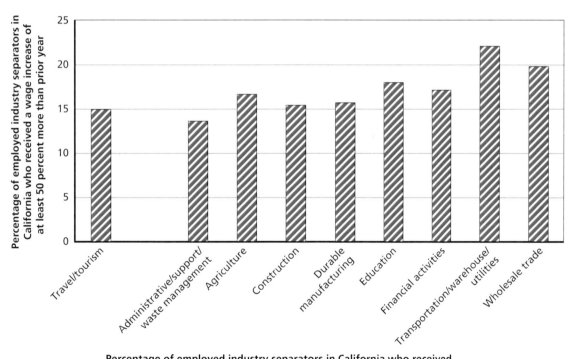

Percentage of employed industry separators in California who received
a wage increase of at least 50 percent more than prior year

SOURCE: SIPP, 2009–2013.

RAND RR1854-3.8

_____

[9]   Prior to calculation of the average, we trim outliers, a typical approach done to account for measurement error at the extremes and the outsized role that the appearance of outliers in a random sample can have on the average (especially true for ratios that may have a very small denominator). We trim by calculating the 99.9th percentile for the *ratio* across all industries and the nation and set any value above the 99.9th percentile equal to the 99.9th percentile. The results do not change in any qualitative way because of this adjustment.

Figure 3.9
Average Annual Change in Wages from Previous Year by Industry, 2010–2013

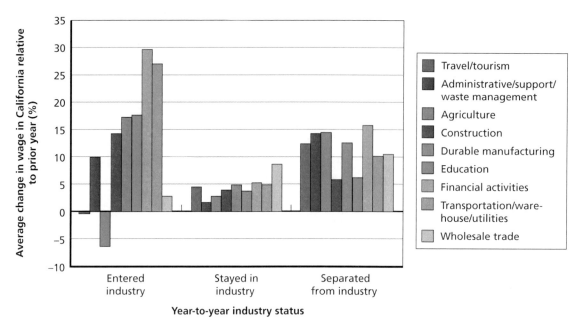

SOURCE: SIPP, 2009–2013.
RAND *RR1854-3.9*

tries.[10] Only California's agriculture industry also averaged a wage decline for entrants. In accordance with Figure 3.8, Figure 3.9's average post-travel/tourism wage change of about a 10-percent wage increase was not unusual.

Figure 3.3's nonpaid-labor-force individuals are excluded from the "Entered Industry" bars in Figure 3.9. Likewise, the "Separated from Industry" average wage-change bars exclude Figure 3.6's nonpaid-labor-force individuals. Figure 3.9 does not control for other factors. We do so in the next section.

Regression Analysis

In this section, we control for the demographic characteristics of the workers in each industry to determine the attributes of the industry relating to employment and wages that are independent of other underlying worker characteristics. First, we investigate the predicted likelihood of an individual who enters the paid labor force to find employment in travel/tourism. To do so, we take the sample of all workers that were not working in the previous year and use a logistic regression to predict the probability of working in California's travel/tourism industry. The control variables include age, educational achievement, gender, number of people in the household, house/apartment ownership or rent, number of children under age 18, race, U.S. citizenship status, speaking an additional language to English, marital status, whether or not ever retired from a job, and whether or not out of the labor force the previous year. We inter-

---

[10] Edith Szivas and Michael Riley, "Tourism Employment During Economic Transition," *Annals of Tourism Research*, Vol. 26, No. 4, October 1999, pp. 747–771.

act age with education status, which allows for the change in predicted travel/tourism entry across different ages to differ by education level. We then predict the likelihood that the worker entered into travel/tourism when he or she found employment. We average across all individuals in the sample to get the average predicted probability at different education levels and ages. Figure 3.10 presents the predicted probability that a person of a given age and educational attainment is working in travel/tourism, conditional on not working in the previous year.[11]

All three trends are decreasing with age: Older workers have been less likely to enter into California's travel/tourism industry relative to other industries after not working the previous year. However, the decrease in the likelihood with respect to age was shallowest for individuals with an educational attainment of high school or less. Those with bachelor's degrees have been more likely to be employed in travel/tourism at all ages than those with some college. These findings suggest that travel/tourism provides a good avenue both for young, low-education individuals entering the paid labor force as well as for those with college degrees.

Next, we regress the average wage-growth ratio investigated in Figure 3.9 on whether a worker stayed in an industry or switched industries, conditional on destination and source industry. We also include a similar set of controls as listed earlier: age, educational achievement, gender, how many others in the household, house/apartment ownership or rent, number of children under age 18, race, U.S. citizenship status, speaking an additional language to English, marital status, and whether or not ever retired from a job. We estimate the difference in the wage-growth ratio from these cases to all other workers (i.e., in industries other than our

Figure 3.10
Logistic Regression Predicted Probabilities of Travel/Tourism Employment

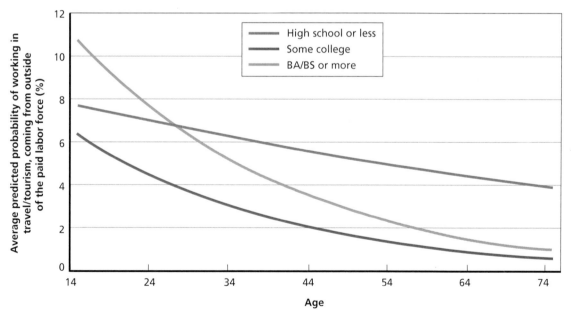

SOURCE: RAND estimate using SIPP, 2009–2013.
RAND RR1854-3.10

---

[11] The level is of secondary importance, as it is relative to the average person on which we estimate the trends. The ranking and trends over age are invariant to the demographics of the person they are tested against, which shift the curves together.

nine industries). Table 3.1 reports the average predicted wage growth for the various types of transitions and industries.

The travel/tourism regression-adjusted average wage increase of 0.113 for separating from the industry means that, controlling for individuals' demographic characteristics, people who separated from travel/tourism to a different industry, on average, experienced an 11.3-percentage point increase in their wages (Table 3.2). Travel/tourism is not an outlier for wage growth staying in the industry or separating from the industry, falling in the middle of the other investigated industries. However, for the industry transitioned into, travel/tourism is one of only two industries (along with agriculture) where the average entrant experienced a slight pay decline, controlling for other variables. This finding is consistent with Figure 3.9.

Summary

California's travel/tourism industry, as we have defined it, has had fairly considerable churn (on the order of 30 percent per annum) both into and out of the industry. Compared with some comparably sized industries in California, travel/tourism has had higher rates of worker entrance and separation than most, although not all, of those industries.

Over 2010–2013, entrants into California's travel/tourism industry were more likely to have come from outside of the paid labor force (unemployed, not in labor force, in school)

Table 3.2
Regression-Adjusted Average Predicted Wage Percentage Increase by Transition

Industry	Entered Industry		Stayed in Industry		Separated from Industry	
	Average Change	Standard Error	Average Change	Standard Error	Average Change	Standard Error
Travel/tourism	−0.039	(0.047)	0.043***	(0.011)	0.113**	(0.049)
Administrative/support/ waste management	0.103**	(0.052)	0.022**	(0.010)	0.160***	(0.063)
Agriculture	−0.066	(0.047)	0.035**	(0.018)	0.158***	(0.058)
Construction	0.139**	(0.059)	0.042***	(0.016)	0.057	(0.054)
Durable manufacturing	0.172***	(0.049)	0.047***	(0.010)	0.136**	(0.058)
Education	0.144***	(0.054)	0.031***	(0.010)	0.063	(0.062)
Financial activities	0.290***	(0.071)	0.047***	(0.015)	0.161**	(0.066)
Transportation/warehouse/ utilities	0.278***	(0.094)	0.054***	(0.013)	0.123**	(0.062)
Wholesale trade	0.012	(0.059)	0.089***	(0.020)	0.106	(0.065)

SOURCE: RAND estimate using SIPP, 2009–2013, with bootstrapped standard errors and p-values.
NOTE: Reported coefficients are based on averaging the predicted wage ratio for each type of transition. Additional control variables in regressions are age, educational achievement, gender, how many others in the household, house/apartment ownership or rent, number of children under age 18, race, the United States citizenship status, speaking an additional language to English, marital status, and whether or not ever retired from a job.
*** Coefficient estimate is significant at the 1-percent level; ** coefficient estimate is significant at the 5-percent level.

than observed for any comparably sized industry in the state. Workers who came from outside of the paid labor force as new entrants into travel/tourism tended to be younger and have a lower educational attainment than workers who came from a different industry, at a higher rate than most comparison industries. However, individuals who separated from travel/tourism had average rates of employment in different industries (i.e., they did not merely separate back to out of the paid labor force at the same higher-than-typical rate as they entered), but elevated rates of attending school.

As is true in other industries, workers who stayed in travel/tourism typically experienced modest wage growth. Fifteen percent of California travel/tourism workers who moved to a job in a different industry increased their hourly wage by more than 50 percent. This sort of favorable outcome is consistent with arguments that travel-related jobs provide a path to upward mobility.

CHAPTER FOUR

Supplemental Analyses

In this chapter, we examine how results change if one uses national (not California-only) data, if one uses a more-inclusive definition of who works in the industry, or if one uses an earlier panel of worker data. The goal of this chapter is to address supplemental questions that help to provide nuance to understanding employed workers in travel/tourism. The chapter examines such questions as the following:

- Does the national travel/tourism industry have trends similar to California's travel/tourism industry's trends?
- Do findings change if one includes California's restaurant industry?
- Do findings change if one uses an earlier SIPP panel?

The explorations in this chapter are separate from one another; we do not combine the analyses.

National-Level Data

We redid all of our analyses using nationwide travel/tourism data (affording us larger sample sizes and, hence, greater precision) and present some of the most insightful findings from these analyses in this section. Do our results for California's travel/tourism industry appear to hold nationwide?

Given our definition of travel/tourism, California's share of nationwide travel/tourism employment has been about 11 percent for the past decade. This share has been rather stable over time, with a slight increase between 2012 and 2014—peaking at 12.4 percent in 2013 and declining somewhat since.

Table 2.1 in Chapter Two showed how the demographics of the California versus the national travel/tourism workforce compare. There, we find across many demographic metrics that California's travel/tourism workers have been similar to their nationwide counterparts, although California's travel/tourism workers have been more likely to be Hispanic or Asian and less likely to be African American.

Table 4.1 additionally reports on the differences in hourly wages, weekly work hours, and frequency of changing jobs. Both the CPS and SIPP report that California's travel/tourism industry has had a slightly higher mean industry wage than the national average (Figure 4.1) during the study period. Of course, the cost of living is also greater than average in California. On the other hand, California's travel/tourism workers work approximately the same number

Table 4.1
Wages, Hours, and Occupation Transition Rates in the SIPP, California and Nationally, 2009–2013

	California		Nation	
	Travel/ Tourism	All Workers	Travel/ Tourism	All Workers
Hourly wage (average)	$19.64	$23.00	$17.61	$20.88
Weekly work hours (average)	35.07	37.47	36.10	37.65
Changed jobs in past year	34.3%	32.8%	39.1%	37.7%
Observations in SIPP	884	18,188	8,761	197,740

SOURCE: SIPP, 2009–2013.

of hours per week as the nation's travel/tourism workers, but they are less likely to change jobs in the past year.

Figure 4.2 shows the wage distribution in travel/tourism in California and nationwide.

California's travel/tourism wage distribution was somewhat higher than the national travel/tourism wage distribution. In California, 28 percent of workers in travel/tourism received less than $10 per hour worked versus 32 percent of national travel/tourism workers. Additionally, in California, about 12 percent of travel/tourism workers (versus 7 percent nationwide) earned more than $35 an hour.

Figure 4.3 compares the California and national average annual entrance into and separation rates from the travel/tourism industry.

Figure 4.1
Average Travel/Tourism Wages Across Data Sources in California and Nationally, 2009–2013

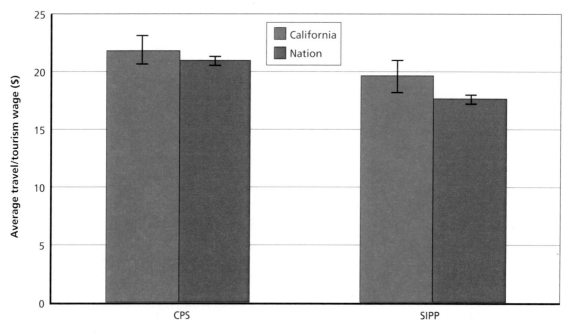

SOURCES: CPS and SIPP, 2009–2013.

RAND RR1854-4.1

Figure 4.2
Distribution of Travel/Tourism Workers' Hourly Wages in California and Nationally, 2009–2013

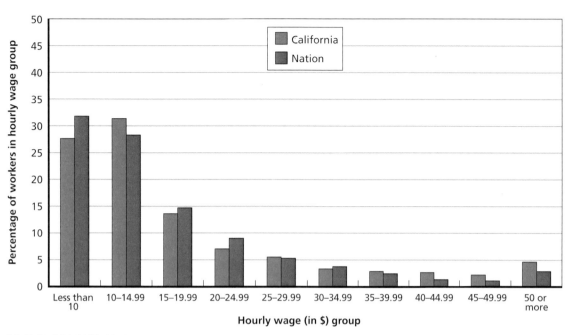

SOURCE: SIPP, 2009–2013.
RAND *RR1854-4.2*

Figure 4.3
Average Annual Percentage of Entrance and Separation in California and Nationally, 2010–2013

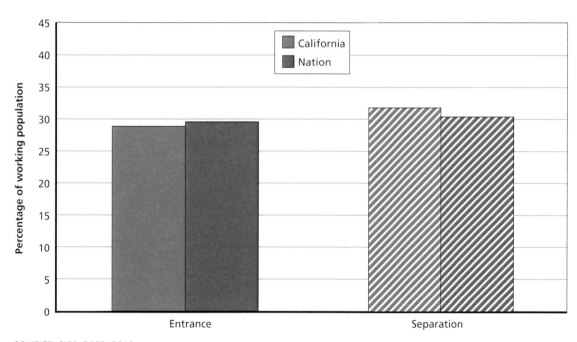

SOURCE: SIPP, 2009–2013.
RAND *RR1854-4.3*

Industry turnover rates have been similar in California and nationally. Note that Figure 4.3 describes annual entrance into and separation rates out of the travel/tourism industry. As one might expect, these travel/tourism industry separation rates are somewhat lower than Table 4.1's "changed jobs in past year" rates (i.e., sometimes people change jobs within the travel/tourism industry).

Figure 4.4 shows that California's travel/tourism industry has drawn more of its new workers from outside of the paid labor force than has been true nationally.

Whereas almost 40 percent of California's new travel/tourism workers came from outside of the paid labor force over 2010–2013, the parallel national percentage was 35 percent. A new travel/tourism worker was more likely to come from the ranks of the unemployed in California than nationwide.

Figure 4.5 shows that somewhat fewer workers (33 percent) in California left the paid labor force after their employment in travel/tourism than was true nationally (34 percent).

Separating California travel/tourism workers were slightly more likely to go back to school and less likely to become unemployed than was true nationally.

Figure 4.6 shows the ratio of new to old hourly average wage for those separating from travel/tourism in California and nationwide during 2009–2013.

About 46 percent of the separators in California experienced at least a 10-percent wage growth in their new industry; the parallel percentage was 41 percent nationally. The percentage of separating travel/tourism workers who received at least 50-percent wage increases in their new industries was almost exactly the same between California (15 percent) and nationally (16 percent).

Figure 4.4
Previous-Year Status of Entrants into Travel/Tourism in California and Nationally, 2010–2013

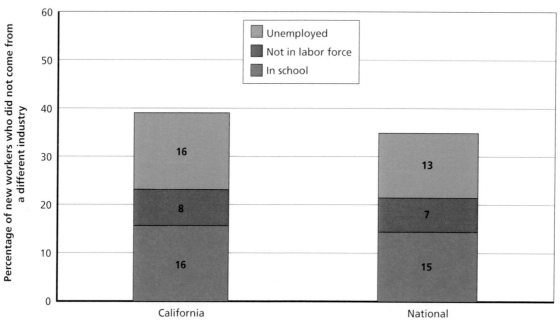

SOURCE: SIPP, 2009–2013.
NOTE: First bar is less than 40 percent because of rounding.
RAND RR1854-4.4

Figure 4.5
Year-After Status of Separators Away from Travel/Tourism in California and Nationally, 2010–2013

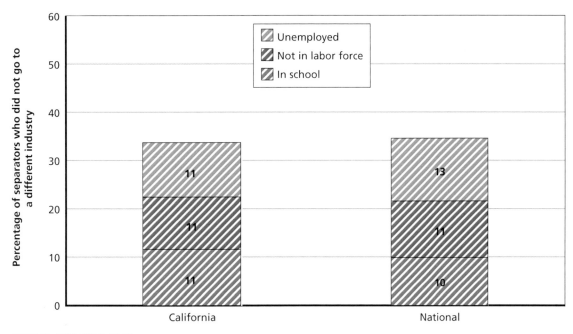

SOURCE: SIPP, 2009–2013.
RAND RR1854-4.5

Figure 4.6
Average Change in Wages from Previous Year of Separators Away from Travel/Tourism in California and Nationally, 2010–2013

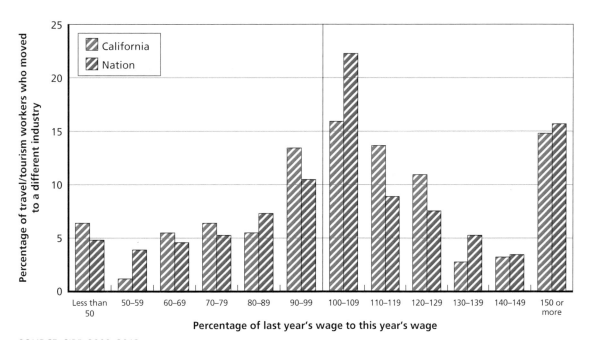

SOURCE: SIPP, 2009–2013.
RAND RR1854-4.6

The larger number of national travel/tourism observations in the SIPP allows us to undertake specific analyses that are not possible with the California-only SIPP. For instance, if we focus on the travel/tourism industry's large-wage-increase alumni (i.e., those individuals noted in Figures 3.7, 3.8, and 4.6 who received at least 50-percent wage increases into their new industry), we find that the California sample size in the SIPP is very small (only 17 observations). However, the sample size is larger (138) if one uses the national pool of high-wage separators, the data source for Table 4.2.

Table 4.2 shows that more highly educated travel/tourism workers nationally have been most likely to receive a large pay increase into their new industry. This is consistent with a portrayal of an individual working in the travel/tourism industry to build up funding for education then leaving the travel/tourism industry for a considerably higher paying position on completion of that education.

A More-Inclusive Definition of the Industry

As noted in Table 1.1 in Chapter One, our baseline analysis excluded workers employed by restaurants (NAICS 7221 and 7222) and drinking places (NAICS 7224) from our definition of the travel/tourism industry. In this analysis, we include these three additional NAICS codes in what we will label "Travel+Restaurants," in contrast with our baseline definition labeled "Travel/Tourism."

Figure 4.7 shows total employment in the industry in California under the two industry definitions.

With the additional categories, the average number of workers in the industry in California for the past two decades increases more than twofold—from about 800,000 to more than two million employees. Workers employed by restaurants and drinking places constitute almost 60 percent of all Travel+Restaurants industry employment. Also, with the more-inclusive definition, the industry was more affected during the 2008–2009 recession years and experienced more rapid recovery from it.

With the more-inclusive industry definition, as shown in Figure 4.8, the industry becomes more youthful.

Table 4.2
Educational Breakdown of Different Categories of National Travel/Tourism Workers, 2009–2013

Education Level	Percentage of All National Travel/ Tourism Workers	Percentage of National Travel/ Tourism Separators	Percentage of National Travel/ Tourism Separators Who Obtained Positions in Another Industry	Percentage of National Travel/ Tourism Separators Who Received at Least a 50-Percent Wage Increase in New Industry
High school or below	36	34	35	20
Some college	40	40	41	42
BA/BS or higher	24	26	24	38

SOURCE: SIPP, 2009–2013.

Figure 4.7
Estimated Employment in California for Two Industry Definitions, 1991–2015

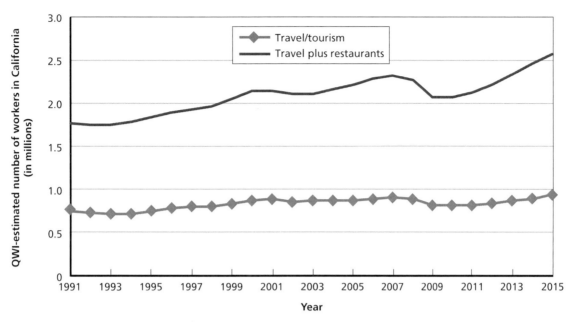

SOURCE: QWI, 1991–2015.

RAND *RR1854-4.7*

Figure 4.8
Distribution of Workers' Ages for Two Industry Definitions, 2009–2013

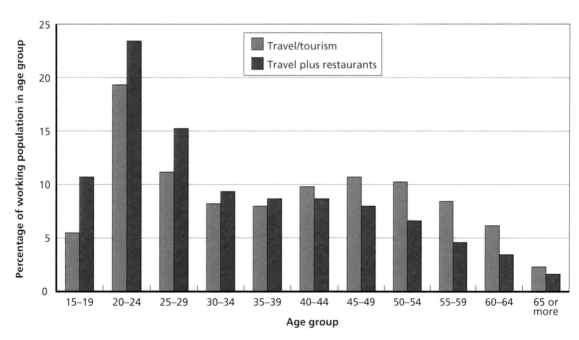

SOURCE: SIPP, 2009–2013.

RAND *RR1854-4.8*

Figure 4.8 shows that including eating and drinking places in the industry shifts the age distribution for the period toward younger people, with 11 percent of workers being younger than 20 and about one-half being younger than 30.

As shown in Figure 4.9, hourly wages of these younger-on-average workers were considerably lower.

Almost one-half of the workers earned less than $10 per hour when we use the expanded definition. Also, about 85 percent of employees earned less than $20 an hour. This change in hourly wage distribution is expected, as many of the restaurant workers were tipped minimum-wage employees.[1]

Figure 4.10 compares the average hours worked under the two industry definitions.

With eating and drinking places included, more workers have been part-time employees—45 percent worked fewer than 35 hours per week as compared with 32 percent for the more-restrictive, baseline definition.

As shown in Figure 4.11, with eating and drinking places included, more workers entered and separated from the industry between 2010 and 2013.

On average, roughly 570,000 individuals entered and separated from the Travel+Restaurants industry across the four years (as compared with a bit more than 200,000 for the more-restrictive, baseline definition of travel/tourism). However, in relative terms, the turnover rate is about the same at 30 percent (i.e., the same percentage of workers transitioned into and out of their industry employment using the two definitions).

Figure 4.9
Distribution of Workers' Hourly Wages for Two Industry Definitions, 2009–2013

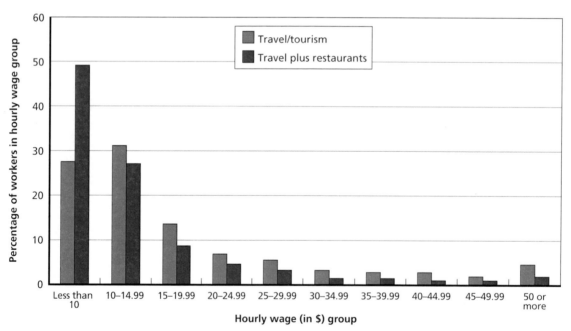

SOURCE: SIPP, 2009–2013.

RAND RR1854-4.9

---

[1]   Although California's minimum wage is the same for both tipped and nontipped employees, for the restaurant industry, the minimum wage has been more binding (i.e., in the SIPP, those in the restaurant industry have been more likely to have wages reported at or below the California minimum wage than in the travel/tourism industry).

Figure 4.10
Distribution of Workers' Weekly Hours of Work for Two Industry Definitions, 2009–2013

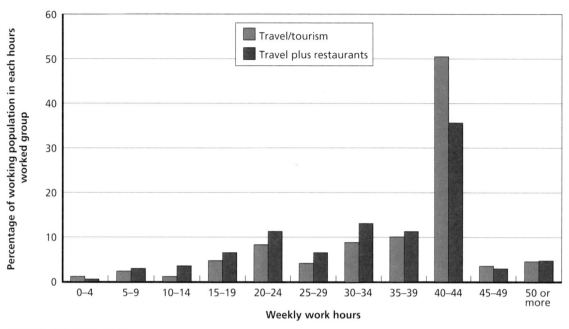

SOURCE: SIPP, 2009–2013.

RAND *RR1854-4.10*

Figure 4.11
Estimated Annual Entrants into and Separators Away for Two Industry Definitions, 2010–2013

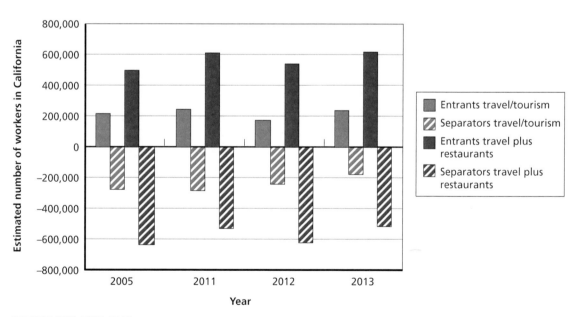

SOURCE: SIPP, 2009–2013.
NOTE: 2009 is the base year for calculations.

RAND *RR1854-4.11*

Figure 4.12 shows, with the more inclusive industry definition, more than one-half of the new workers for 2010–2013 came from outside of the paid labor force.

The difference between the two bars in Figure 4.12 is solely in the percentage of those who were in school the year before: 28 percent for the inclusive definition and 16 percent for the more restrictive, baseline definition.

Figure 4.13 compares the year-after status of separators under the two industry definitions.

With the expanded Travel+Restaurants industry definition, more industry separators were not in the paid labor force the year after leaving the industry, with marked increases in both the percentage returning to school and the percentage unemployed.

Figure 4.14 compares separators' wages to their last travel/tourism wage across the two industry definitions.

Wage dynamics for the two industry definitions have been similar—slightly more than one-half of the separators from Travel+Restaurants experienced at least 10-percent wage growth in their next job as compared with 46 percent for the baseline travel/tourism definition. But with restaurant workers included, 19 percent of separators employed in a different industry moved to much more lucrative jobs (150 percent or more of previous wage), a higher percentage than that with the baseline definition (15 percent).

Use of the 2004–2007 SIPP

Our baseline analysis uses the 2009–2013 SIPP. As shown in Figure 2.1 in Chapter Two, that time restriction (intrinsic to SIPP, not something we chose) is unfortunate in that it misses

Figure 4.12
Previous-Year Status of Entrants for Two Industry Definitions, 2010–2013

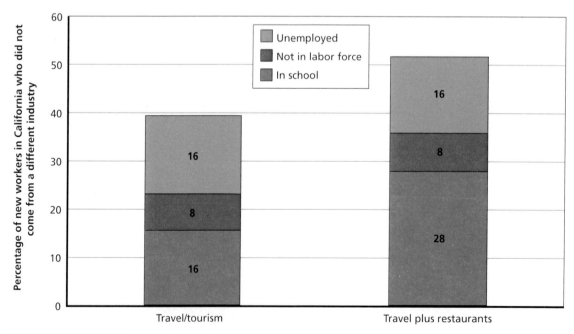

SOURCE: SIPP, 2009–2013.
NOTE: First bar is less than 40 percent because of rounding.
RAND RR1854-4.12

Figure 4.13
Year-After Status of Separators for Two Industry Definitions, 2010–2013

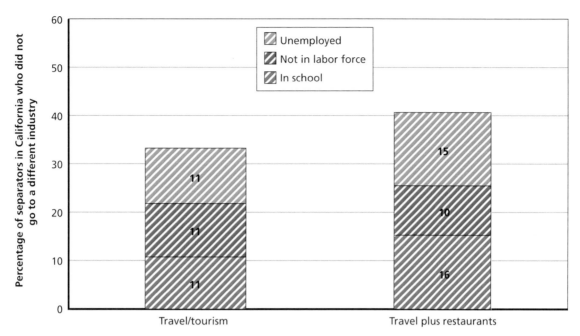

SOURCE: SIPP, 2009–2013.
RAND RR1854-4.13

Figure 4.14
Average Change in Wages from Previous Year for Separators for Two Industry Definitions, 2010–2013

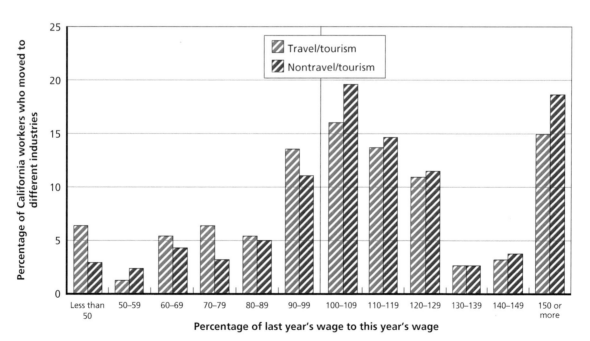

SOURCE: SIPP, 2009–2013.
RAND RR1854-4.14

the sharp drop in industry employment observed between 2008 and 2009. The earlier SIPP panel does not help us with that omission, as it ran 2004–2007. Nevertheless, in this section, we evaluate whether and to what extent our findings would be different looking at this earlier SIPP panel. Figure 4.15 shows the two SIPP panels' estimated levels of travel/tourism employment in California in 2004–2007 then, with the newer panel, 2009–2013.

There was a sizable increase in employment in California's travel/tourism industry in 2007. We do not see such a marked employment level change in the industry in our later, baseline SIPP panel.

Figure 4.16 shows estimates of annual entrants into and separators away from California's travel/tourism across the two panels.

During 2005–2007, substantially more people entered the industry than separated away from it. In the peak year, 2007, more than 300,000 new hires came into travel/tourism and fewer than 200,000 separated away from it (i.e., California's travel/tourism industry grew by about 100,000 new workers right before the recession). On average, there were 7 percent more new hires into the industry than separators between 2005 and 2007. Our baseline study period of 2010–2013 showed a much more static employment level in the industry.

In the earlier SIPP, new travel/tourism workers were more likely to come from other industries, as shown in Figure 4.17.

Twenty-seven percent of workers new to California's travel/tourism were unemployed, in school, or otherwise not in the labor force before the recession versus almost 40 percent in the later SIPP. After 2009, the industry's new hires were much more likely to come from the ranks of the unemployed. This may be explained by the fact that California's average unemploy-

Figure 4.15
Two SIPP Panels' Estimates of Annual Travel/Tourism Employment Levels in California

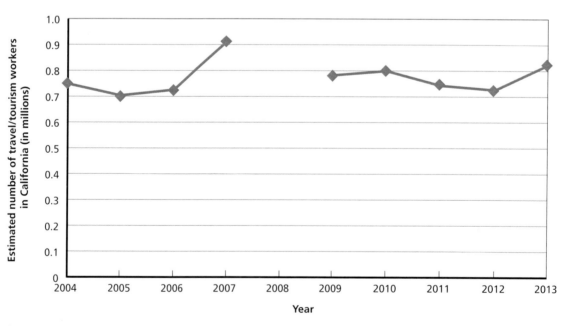

SOURCES: SIPP, 2004–2007, 2009–2013.
RAND RR1854-4.15

Figure 4.16
Estimated Annual Entrants into and Separators Away from California's Travel/Tourism Industry,
2005–2007 and 2010–2013

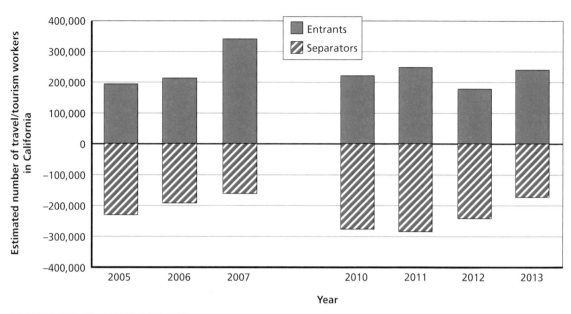

SOURCES: SIPP, 2004–2007, 2009–2013.
NOTE: 2004 and 2009 are base years for calculations.
RAND RR1854-4.16

Figure 4.17
Previous-Year Status of Entrants, Two SIPP Panels

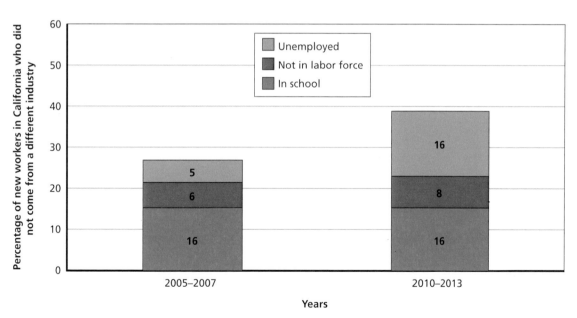

SOURCES: SIPP, 2004–2007, 2009–2013.
NOTE: 2004 and 2009 are base years for calculations. Second bar is less than 40 percent because of rounding.
RAND RR1854-4.17

ment rate between 2004 and 2006 was considerably lower, 5.5 percent, than the state's average unemployment rate between 2009 and 2012, 11.3 percent.[2]

Figure 4.18 shows previous-year statuses of entrants into the comparison industries in the earlier SIPP panel.

Of the comparison industries during the earlier SIPP panel, agriculture, education, and admin/support drew substantially more of their new workers from outside the paid labor force than travel/tourism did. This result diverges from 2010–2013's Figure 3.3 in Chapter Three, in which travel/tourism drew the greatest percentage of its new workers from outside of the paid labor force across the nine industries.

Figure 4.19 compares the year-after status of separators across the two panels. It shows that, on average, fewer travel/tourism workers left the paid labor force between 2005 and 2007 than between 2010 and 2013—22 percent versus 33 percent. Of those who left their paid employment, more travel/tourism alumni were likely to go back to school or drop out of the labor force in the later panel than in the earlier panel. As noted, California's overall economy performed much better during the earlier panel than during the later, baseline, panel.

Finally, Figure 4.20 shows the ratio of the new hourly to the old hourly wage for the separators from the travel/tourism industry for the two panels.

In the earlier SIPP panel, 51 percent of travel/tourism workers experienced at least 10-percent wage growth in their new industry versus 46 percent in the later panel. Also, about

Figure 4.18
Previous-Year Status of Entrants into Comparison Industries in California, 2005–2007

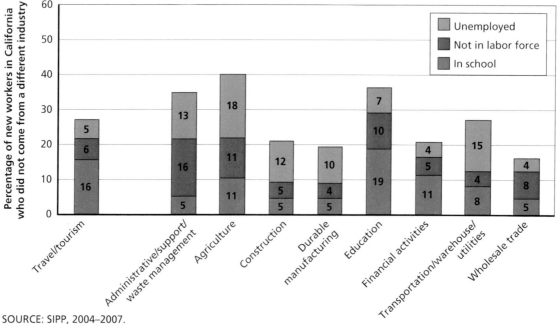

SOURCE: SIPP, 2004–2007.
NOTE: 2004 is the base year for calculations. "Financial activities" is more than 20 percent because of rounding. RAND RR1854-4.18

2   U.S. Department of Labor, Bureau of Labor Statistics, "Databases, Tables, and Calculators by Subject," undated(a).

Figure 4.19
Year-After Status of Separators Away from Travel/Tourism Industries in California, Two SIPP Panels

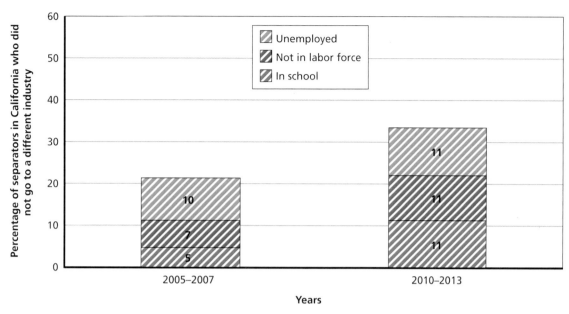

SOURCES: SIPP, 2004–2007, 2009–2013.
NOTE: 2004 and 2009 are base years for calculations.
RAND RR1854-4.19

Figure 4.20
Average Change in Wages for Industry Separators from Previous Year in California Travel/Tourism, Two SIPP Panels

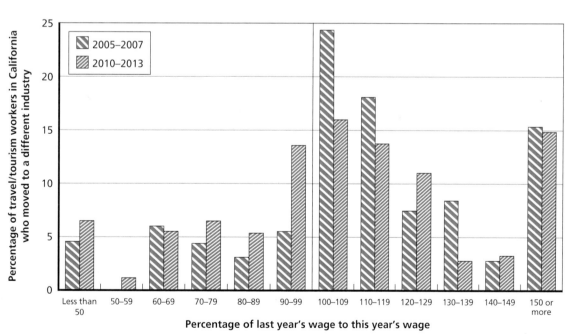

SOURCES: SIPP, 2004–2007, 2009–2013.
RAND RR1854-4.20

15 percent of industry separators moved to considerably higher-paid jobs (150 percent or more of previous wage) in the earlier panel, almost the same percentage as seen in the later panel.

Summary

Across many demographic metrics, California travel/tourism workers have been similar to their nationwide counterparts, although California's workers have been more likely to be Hispanic or Asian. California's travel/tourism industry has drawn a larger percentage of its new workers from outside of the paid labor force than has been true nationally.

Adding eating and drinking places workers to California's travel/tourism industry changes the industry's demographics considerably, more than doubling the industry's employment level. With the more-inclusive industry definition, its workers were younger (one-half being younger than 30) and lower paid (one-half earning less than $10 per hour). With the more-inclusive industry definition, more than one-half of the new workers came from outside the paid labor force over 2010–2013. When one includes restaurant-industry workers, the phenomenon of alumni moving to more-lucrative positions is even more common, with 19 percent of alumni who moved to employment in a different industry receiving a wage increase of 50 percent or more.

Whereas almost 40 percent of entrants into California's travel/tourism industry came from outside of the paid labor force in the 2010–2013 period, only about one-quarter came from outside of the paid labor force over 2005–2007. The difference lies in a sharply lower number of unemployed individuals joining travel/tourism in the 2005–2007 period, which may reflect the fact that California's average unemployment rate between 2004 and 2006 was 5.5 percent, while the state's average unemployment rate between 2009 and 2012 was 11.3 percent. Although the travel/tourism industry distinguished itself over 2010–2013 for hiring nonpaid labor force individuals, its performance on this metric was more typical compared with other industries over 2005–2007, when the state's economy was performing better.

CHAPTER FIVE

Discussion

One of our questions at the outset of this study was: Who works in the travel/tourism industry in California? Indeed, that question has no straightforward answer. Tourism affects hundreds of thousands of workers across a variety of industries in the state.

However, in that we wanted to trace careers of individuals who work in California's travel/tourism industry, we had to draw boundaries as to who "counts" as being employed in the industry. We ended up with a conservative tally (noninclusive of restaurant and retail industry workers) of about 800,000 individuals working in California in what we define to be the travel/tourism industry.

Workers in the industry span a variety of ages, with an overrepresentation of workers in their early 20s. About one-third works fewer than 35 hours per week. Hourly wages in California's travel/tourism industry are often low, but there also are some high-wage earners in the industry. We began to see that there were broadly speaking two types of workers in travel/tourism: long-term workers who worked more consistently in the industry and were older and more likely to work more hours, and had higher wages, and transitional workers who came in and out of the travel/tourism industry, who are likely benefiting from easier likelihood of transitioning into travel/tourism from outside the paid labor force.

Having identified individuals we defined to work in California's travel/tourism industry, we then examined how their careers evolve. California's travel/tourism industry has had roughly 30-percent annual entrance and separation rates (i.e., on average, workers have stayed in the industry for about three years). Relative to other comparably sized industries in the state, new hires into California's travel/tourism industry have been more likely to come from outside of the paid labor force. This effect was attenuated in 2005–2007, when California's unemployment rate was lower. Those coming from outside the paid labor force tended to be younger and less likely to hold bachelor's degrees than those coming from other industries, at a rate higher than most of our comparison industries. Most California travel/tourism industry separators moved on to employment in other industries, although a sizable percentage returned to school.

Whereas entrants into California's travel/tourism industry have been disproportionately likely to come from outside of the paid labor force, individuals separating from California's travel/tourism industry often "look like" other industries' separators. California travel/tourism separators have had typical rates of employment in a different industry and have had typical rates of receiving a large pay increase into a new industry.

One interpretation, therefore, is that California's travel/tourism industry has, in addition to being a long-term career path for many individuals, also served as a gateway into paid employment for individuals not currently in the paid labor force. When paired with additional education, this path can result in high wage growth for separating workers and stable career pathways for individuals who choose to have longer careers in travel/tourism. Travel/tourism industry employment may be especially valuable during difficult economic times when workers might otherwise be unemployed.

Economic Multipliers: What Are They and What Do They Mean?

To help us assess the effects of travel/tourism on California's economy, we examined the literature on economic multipliers (i.e., how spending in a category such as travel/tourism can multiply through the broader economy).

There is considerable literature on economic multipliers, to assess the effect of both travel/tourism and many other types of economic activity.[1] In this appendix, we discuss what we have learned in part to raise concerns about this analytic approach.

Research that looks at the economic impact of tourism often employs one of the two types of techniques: IO analysis[2] and/or computable general equilibrium (CGE).[3] These two models are fundamentally different in their setup, assumptions, and estimated results, although CGE may yield the same output as an IO model under specific assumptions. CGE modeling is also viewed as broader in scope and demanding more resources (i.e., more parameters to estimate) to implement.[4]

IO methodology has a number of basic assumptions, such as direct links between an industry of interest and other parts of the economy as well as unlimited flow of resources. An underlying mechanism of IO modeling is deterministically tracing the effect of an initial stimulus throughout the economic system.[5] Consequently, the IO method assumes that there is no effect of price changes (direct or indirect) on either industry inputs or output—that is, there are no substitution effects and no scarcity.

CGE models move beyond IO analysis in that they design markets that are cleared by an equilibrium price. Thus, in contrast to IO models, by modeling the underlying behavior of the

---

[1] Keating et al. noted extensive use of IO multipliers to assess the economic impacts of defense spending (Edward G. Keating, Irina Danescu, Dan Jenkins, James Black, Robert Murphy, Deborah Peetz, and Sarah H. Bana, *The Economic Consequences of Investing in Shipbuilding: Case Studies in the United States and Sweden*, Santa Monica, Calif.: RAND Corporation, RR-1036-AUS, 2011). See also James Hosek, Aviva Litovitz, and Adam C. Resnick, *How Much Does Military Spending Add to Hawaii's Economy?* Santa Monica, Calif.: RAND Corporation, TR-996-OSD, 2011.

[2] John E. Fletcher, "Input-Output Analysis and Tourism Impact Studies," *Annals of Tourism Research*, Vol. 16, No. 4, 1989, pp. 514–529; Helen Briassoulis, "Methodological Issues: Tourism Input-Output Analysis," *Annals of Tourism Research*, Vol. 18, No. 3, 1991, pp. 485–495; Rebecca L. Johnson, and Eric Moore, "Tourism Impact Estimation," *Annals of Tourism Research*, Vol. 20, No. 2, 1993, pp. 279–288.

[3] Deying Zhou, John F. Yanagida, Ujjayant Chakravorty, and PingSun Leung, "Estimating Economic Impacts from Tourism," *Annals of Tourism Research*, Vol. 24, No. 1, 1997, pp. 76–89.

[4] Larry Dwyer, Peter Forsyth, and Ray Spurr, "Evaluating Tourism's Economic Effects: New and Old Approaches," *Tourism Management*, Vol. 25, No. 3, June 2004, pp. 307–317.

[5] Adam Blake, Ramesh Durbarry, M. Thea Sinclair, and Guntur Sugiyarto, "Modelling Tourism and Travel Using Tourism Satellite Accounts and Tourism Policy and Forecasting Models," discussion paper, Tourism and Travel Research Institute, January 2001.

economic agents who incorporate prices into their decisionmaking, CGE is formulated and solved for all the markets and sectors simultaneously. In practice, CGE-estimated multipliers are usually smaller than those of IO models—that is, growth in one industry often has negative (displacement) effects on other industries.[6]

RIMS Estimates for Travel/Tourism in California

The Regional Input-Output Modeling System (RIMS) was developed by the BEA in the 1970s "as a tool to help economists analyze the potential effects of economic activities on regional economies."[7] RIMS is an implementation of the IO method, tailored specifically to regional analysis in the U.S. context. RIMS provides estimates of total cumulative effects of demand on output, earnings, and employment.

Suppose a tourist spends $100 on accommodation in California. RIMS estimates that, on average, the hotel where he or she stays will spend $40 on goods and services from other industries and $31 compensating employees. Twenty dollars goes to what RIMS terms "gross operating surplus" (i.e., reinvesting in the business like paying the mortgage). About $9 is paid in taxes, RIMS estimates. This hotel spending, in turn, leads to more spending by the affected recipient industries and employees (i.e., it multiplies).

Cumulating these effects, RIMS estimates that an extra dollar spent at a hotel in California results in $1.97 in total economic output in the state and $0.58 in additional wages paid in the state. RIMS also estimates that 15.6 jobs in the state are created per $1 million in hotel receipts.

We can do similar calculations for other subcategories of travel/tourism and, in turn, aggregate them as presented in Table A.1. Looking more generally across all of the categories we define as encompassing travel/tourism, RIMS estimates that an extra dollar spent in the category in California results in a total of $2.14 in total economic output in the state and $0.65 in additional wages in the state. RIMS also estimates that 17.01 jobs in the state are created per $1 million in travel/tourism spending.

Table A.1's RIMS multipliers (as well as Table A.2's) are based on the 2007 benchmark IO table for the nation and 2013 regional data. We received our data pull in March 2016.

Using a similar model (Impact Analysis for Planning [IMPLAN] rather than RIMS), Dean Runyan Associates finds a California travel spending–earnings multiplier of 2.01, very close to our RIMS weighted average of 2.14.[8]

We can likewise estimate California RIMS multipliers for the eight comparison industries as shown in Table A.2.

Travel/tourism's output multiplier of 2.14 is broadly similar to the other industries', ranking fourth largest of the nine. A considerable contributor to the magnitude of RIMS output multipliers is how much funding leaks out of a state. Previous research notes that tourism earnings–multiplier estimates tend to be higher in larger regions and countries with self-sufficient economies and lower in smaller regions and countries where earnings leak out of the economy

---

[6] Zhou et al., 1997; Dwyer, Forsyth, and Spurr, 2004.

[7] For an overview of RIMS, see U.S. Department of Commerce, *RIMS II: An Essential Tool for Regional Developers and Planners*, Washington, D.C., December 2013.

[8] Dean Runyan Associates, 2015.

Table A.1
Estimated California Travel/Tourism RIMS Multipliers

	Output	Earnings	Employment (Jobs per $1 Million in Spending)
Traveler accommodation	1.97	0.58	15.57
Amusements, gambling, and recreation	2.07	0.59	21.66
Air transportation	2.02	0.48	8.85
Rail transportation	2.02	0.52	8.63
Water transportation	2.22	0.50	9.20
Transit and ground passenger transportation	2.42	0.86	24.52
Other transportation and support activities	2.23	0.77	16.41
Performing arts, spectator sports, museums	2.25	0.71	20.28
Weighted average	2.14	0.65	17.01

Table A.2
Estimated RIMS Multipliers for Different Industries in California

	Output	Earnings	Employment (Jobs per $1 Million in Spending)
Travel/tourism	2.14	0.65	17.01
Administrative/support/waste management	2.17	0.82	22.78
Agriculture	1.95	0.56	12.24
Construction	2.12	0.70	14.54
Durable manufacturing	1.99	0.54	9.91
Education	2.28	0.83	22.72
Financial activities	2.20	0.64	12.36
Transportation/warehouse/utilities	1.97	0.51	9.92
Wholesale trade	1.98	0.62	11.50

through importing goods and services to satisfy tourism demand.[9] Not surprisingly, Grau

---

[9] Stephen Wanhill, "The Measurement of Tourist Income Multipliers," *Tourism Management*, Vol. 15, No. 4, August 1994, pp. 281–283; Endre Horvath and Douglas C. Frechtling, "Estimating the Multiplier Effects of Tourism Expenditures on a Local Economy Through a Regional Input-Output Model," *Journal of Travel Research*, Vol. 37, No. 4, May 1999, pp. 324–332; Stephen Pratt, "Economic Linkages and Impacts Across the TALC," *Annals of Tourism Research*, Vol. 38, No. 2, 2011, pp. 630–650.

reports lower IO IMPLAN travel-related multipliers of 1.4–1.7 for Montana.[10] That state has a much smaller economy than California's, so spending leaves the state more quickly.

Concerns with RIMS Estimates

RIMS, IMPLAN, and similar IO models make assumptions that probably do not hold.

Dwyer, Forsyth, and Spurr present a trenchant critique of usage of IO multiplier analyses to make estimates of the economic effects of changes in tourism expenditures.[11] Most directly, RIMS calculations assume that an industry can grow with no changes in wages and no adverse effects on other industries. De facto, this assumes that new workers come from outside of the current paid labor force (e.g., unemployed, just out of school, new to the region, retirees), not lured away from other industries in the region, unless those departures are immediately replaced from outside of the region's paid labor force.

A more accurate estimate of the effect of increased activity by an industry would consider that some of its new employees previously held different jobs. What happened to the industries from which these new workers came? Have output and employment in those industries declined? Do wages increase to attract the marginal person not working, or is there a decrease in employment in the industry the worker left?

A key question, therefore, as we evaluate the economic effect of travel/tourism, is what the industry's workers might otherwise be doing.

If, absent their travel industry jobs, they would be unemployed, retired, or otherwise not in the paid labor force, a RIMS-estimated multiplier may be appropriate.

If, absent their travel industry jobs, they would be working in a different industry, the question then becomes whether they are replaced in that industry and, if so, by whom and how quickly. RIMS-multiplier validity depends on whether the worker is replaced one-for-one in the former industry, without a substantial lag, by someone who would otherwise not be in the paid labor force.

These sorts of concerns with RIMS-multiplier estimates motivate use of CGE models. A CGE model introduces additional parameters (e.g., characterizing labor supply elasticity) that address an IO model's limitations. Appropriately calibrating such parameters would be challenging, although our analyses with SIPP data could be used toward that end. The development of a CGE model of travel/tourism in California was beyond the scope of our project.

---

[10] Kara Grau, "2015 Nonresident Visitation, Expenditures and Economic Impact Estimates: Estimates by Full Year, Quarters, Trip Purposes, and International Visitors," *Institute for Tourism and Recreation Research Publications*, paper 333, April 26, 2016.

[11] Dwyer, Forsyth, and Spurr, 2004.

References

Blake, Adam, Ramesh Durbarry, M. Thea Sinclair, and Guntur Sugiyarto, "Modelling Tourism and Travel Using Tourism Satellite Accounts and Tourism Policy and Forecasting Models," discussion paper, Tourism and Travel Research Institute, January 2001.

Boudarbat, Brahim, and Marie Connolly, "The Gender Wage Gap Among Recent Post-Secondary Graduates in Canada: A Distributional Approach," *Canadian Journal of Economics/Revue canadienne d'économique*, Vol. 46, No. 3, August 2013, pp. 1037–1065.

Bowlus, Audra J., and Shannon N. Seitz, "Search Friction in the U.S. Labor Market: Equilibrium Estimates from the PSID," *Contributions to Economic Analysis*, Vol. 243, 2000, pp. 145–170.

Briassoulis, Helen, "Methodological Issues: Tourism Input-Output Analysis," *Annals of Tourism Research*, Vol. 18, No. 3, 1991, pp. 485–495.

Dean Runyan Associates, *California Travel Industry: Business Characteristics, Employees, Wages*, Portland, Oreg., May 2013.

———, *California Travel Impacts, 1992–2014p*, Portland, Oreg., April 2015.

———, *California Travel Impacts by County, 1992–2015p*, Portland, Oreg., April 2016.

Delgado, M., M. E. Porter, and S. Stern, *Defining Clusters of Related Industries*, June 2014. As of December 22, 2016:
http://www.nber.org/data-appendix/w20375/Technical_Appendix_DPS_Jun2014.pdf

Dwyer, Larry, Peter Forsyth, and Ray Spurr, "Evaluating Tourism's Economic Effects: New and Old Approaches," *Tourism Management*, Vol. 25, No. 3, June 2004, pp. 307–317.

Fletcher, John E., "Input-Output Analysis and Tourism Impact Studies," *Annals of Tourism Research*, Vol. 16, No. 4, 1989, pp. 514–529.

Frechtling, Douglas C., "The Tourism Satellite Account: A Primer," *Annals of Tourism Research*, Vol. 37, No. 1, January 2010, pp. 136–153.

Grau, Kara, "2015 Nonresident Visitation, Expenditures and Economic Impact Estimates: Estimates by Full Year, Quarters, Trip Purposes, and International Visitors," *Institute for Tourism and Recreation Research Publications*, paper 333, April 26, 2016. As of June 27, 2016:
http://scholarworks.umt.edu/itrr_pubs/333/

Horvath, Endre, and Douglas C. Frechtling, "Estimating the Multiplier Effects of Tourism Expenditures on a Local Economy Through a Regional Input-Output Model," *Journal of Travel Research*, Vol. 37, No. 4, May 1999, pp. 324–332.

Hosek, James, Aviva Litovitz, and Adam C. Resnick, *How Much Does Military Spending Add to Hawaii's Economy?* Santa Monica, Calif.: RAND Corporation, TR-996-OSD, 2011. As of December 12, 2016:
http://www.rand.org/pubs/technical_reports/TR996.html

Johnson, Rebecca L., and Eric Moore, "Tourism Impact Estimation," *Annals of Tourism Research*, Vol. 20, No. 2, 1993, pp. 279–288.

Keating, Edward G., Irina Danescu, Dan Jenkins, James Black, Robert Murphy, Deborah Peetz, and Sarah H. Bana, *The Economic Consequences of Investing in Shipbuilding: Case Studies in the United States and Sweden*, Santa Monica, Calif.: RAND Corporation, RR-1036-AUS, 2011. As of December 12, 2016:
http://www.rand.org/pubs/research_reports/RR1036.html

Lacher, R. Geoffrey, and Chi-Ok Oh, "Is Tourism a Low Income Industry? Evidence from Three Coastal Regions," *Journal of Travel Research*, Vol. 51, No. 4, July 2012, pp. 464–472.

Lise, Jeremy, Nao Sudo, Michio Suzuki, Ken Yamada, and Tomoaki Yamada, "Wage, Income and Consumption Inequality in Japan, 1981–2008: From Boom to Lost Decades," *Review of Economic Dynamics*, Vol. 17, No. 4, 2014, pp. 582–612.

Lucas, Rosemary, *Employment Relations in the Hospitality and Tourism Industries*, London: Routledge, 2004.

McKenzie, David, Caroline Theoharides, and Dean Yang, "Distortions in the International Migrant Labor Market: Evidence from Filipino Migration and Wage Responses to Destination Country Economic Shocks," *American Economic Journal: Applied Economics*, Vol. 6, No. 2, 2014, pp. 49–75.

Osborne, Jason W., and Amy Overbay, "The Power of Outliers (and Why Researchers Should Always Check for Them)," *Practical Assessment, Research, and Evaluation*, Vol. 9, No. 6, March 2004, pp. 1–12.

Pratt, Stephen, "Economic Linkages and Impacts Across the TALC," *Annals of Tourism Research*, Vol. 38, No. 2, 2011, pp. 630–650.

State of California, Department of Industrial Relations, "History of California Minimum Wage," January 1, 2016. As of January 6, 2016:
http://www.dir.ca.gov/iwc/minimumwagehistory.htm

Szivas, Edith, and Michael Riley, "Tourism Employment During Economic Transition," *Annals of Tourism Research*, Vol. 26, No. 4, October 1999, pp. 747–771.

Szivas, Edith, Michael Riley, and David Airey, "Labor Mobility into Tourism: Attraction and Satisfaction," *Annals of Tourism Research*, Vol. 30, No. 1, 2003, pp. 64–76.

Terek, Milan, and Matús Tibenský, "Outliers and Some Non-Traditional Measures of Location in Analysis of Wages," *European Scientific Journal*, Vol. 1, September 2014, pp. 480–486.

Tourism Economics, "California Travel and Tourism Outlook" briefing, February 2016.

United Nations, *Tourism Satellite Account: Recommended Methodological Framework 2008*, Luxembourg, Madrid, New York, and Paris: Department of Economic and Social Affairs, Statistics Division, Studies in Methods Series F, No. 80/Rev. 1, 2010. As of June 26, 2016:
http://unstats.un.org/unsd/publication/Seriesf/SeriesF_80rev1e.pdf

U.S. Census Bureau, *Quarterly Workforce Indicators 101*, Washington, D.C., December 18, 2015. As of June 28, 2016:
http://lehd.ces.census.gov/doc/QWI_101.pdf

U.S. Department of Commerce, Bureau of Economic Analysis, *RIMS II: An Essential Tool for Regional Developers and Planners*, Washington, D.C., December 2013. As of June 26, 2016:
https://www.bea.gov/regional/pdf/rims/rimsii_user_guide.pdf

———, "Broad Growth Across States in 2014," Washington, D.C., June 10, 2015. As of September 5, 2016:
http://www.bea.gov/newsreleases/regional/gdp_state/gsp_newsrelease.htm

U.S. Department of Labor, Bureau of Labor Statistics, "Databases, Tables, and Calculators by Subject," undated(a). As of November 18, 2016:
http://www.bls.gov/data/

———, "Economy at a Glance: California," undated(b). As of September 5, 2016:
http://www.bls.gov/eag/eag.ca.htm

———, "Administrative and Support and Waste Management and Remediation Services: NAICS 56," January 6, 2017a. As of September 6, 2016:
http://www.bls.gov/iag/tgs/iag56.htm

————, "Support Activities for Transportation: NAICS 488," January 6, 2017b. As of October 2, 2016:
http://www.bls.gov/iag/tgs/iag488.htm

U.S. Travel Association, *Fast Forward: Travel Creates Opportunities and Launches Careers*, Washington, D.C., 2012. As of June 26, 2016:
https://www.ustravel.org/sites/default/files/Media%20Root/e-Fast_Forward.pdf

————, *The Economic Review of Travel in America: 2015 Edition*, Washington, D.C., January 2016a.

————, *The Impact of Travel on State Economies: 2015 Edition*, Washington, D.C., January 2016b.

Wanhill, Stephen, "The Measurement of Tourist Income Multipliers," *Tourism Management*, Vol. 15, No. 4, August 1994, pp. 281–283.

Whalley, Alexander, "Education and Labor Market Risk: Understanding the Role of Data Cleaning," *Economics of Education Review*, Vol. 30, No. 3, 2011, pp. 528–545.

Zhou, Deying, John F. Yanagida, Ujjayant Chakravorty, and PingSun Leung, "Estimating Economic Impacts from Tourism," *Annals of Tourism Research*, Vol. 24, No. 1, 1997, pp. 76–89.